QUIET LEADERSHIP

Change Your World With A Whisper

KAREN GROSZ

Quiet Leadership

FROM READERS OF THE PRE-RELEASE BOOK

As I read each chapter, I was reminded how little I really know about Leadership ... and how much I want to be a better, now Quiet, Leader. ~Bill Schomburg

Karen has a way of slipping thunderous, world-changing thoughts into a simple story. Quiet Leadership is about learning to listen for and lean into those thoughts, wherever they find you in life. ~Matt Bartenhagen

Karen paints a picture of leadership with vivid storytelling giving the reader a roadmap to being the kind of leader that can change the world with a whisper rather than shouting from rooftops. The real-world examples of regular people leading collaborative teams is inspiring and shows that anyone can make a difference if they lead with a quiet understanding. ~ Jasmine Hansen

I learned long ago, one way to quiet an audience is to lower your voice, not raise it. In "Quiet Leadership," Karen Grosz takes that to the next level. Through wonderful anecdotes and stories, Karen will take you on a journey to a new approach to leading, whether it be a youth organization as I volunteer with, or a multi-million dollar corporation. Open the covers, pick a chapter, and begin to "quiet down!" ~ Paul Mossberg

I needed this book. An eye-opener on listening to hear, and pausing to see. Quiet Leadership changes you with one memorable story after another of humans leading lives with great impact and grace. ~Kris Rocky

Reflection, improvement, movement and motivation all come to mind as I was reading these well-written stories this weekend! I'm very excited for what's to come! ~Steven Peterman

Exactly what I need! I can be verbally quiet, but, the brain continues to talk inside my head.....love your mission. ~Kristy Samaria

Karen knows how to take the written word, create engagement and make it simple to apply in the real world of leadership. Instead of presenting the material in a technical, traditional way, Karen takes the material and captivates the reader with her witty, amusing, and brilliant stories. These stories are relatable to the everyday person and to the Fortune 500 CEO. I have read a comprehensive amount of leadership books in my career and Karen's Quiet Leadership is one of my new favorites. It is an easy-to-read, process, and implement kind of book. Once you start, you will easily be hooked in and keep reading. Dr. Victoria Arneson

Epic insight on quiet Leadership! ~ Terri Todd

I love the perspective you always share and make me adjust how I see, listen and hear things. ~ Debbie Bailey

Quiet Leadership is what I'm striving for. Thank you for having me be part of this. ~ Tina Roberts

These excerpts beautifully weave together heart-warming stories and pragmatic advice in a meaningful, relatable way! I most related to the Two Drunk and A Mayor story. As a nomad, establishing community is so important, and surrounding ourselves with all sorts of people is what makes life delicious! ~Kim Lewis

As I succumb to the words of Karen and the storytelling and humor that has transformed us. I am awestruck at Karen's ability to be a curious observer of others seeing in them the things that they can't even see themselves. Leadership is multi-faceted and deep and Karen's personal descriptions are a breath of fresh air in the 'quick fix' 'how to' 'next course' society that leaders find themselves in today. ~Sheridan Cotrell

In Quiet Leadership, Karen Grosz uses stories and humor to highlight the qualities of effective, collaborative leadership. By describing the everyday heroes around us, she shows us how we too can be those heroes, quietly and humbly shaping our world to be better through our everyday actions. Read it

*for inspiration for achieving your big visions or simply to enjoy the stories.
Barbara Cromwell*

*I can honestly say I love the Quiet Leadership concept. You have painted
some really entertaining stories here that get your message across. I
appreciate you allowing me to be a little part of your book launch. We need
more people leading for the right reasons and I love that you are cultivating
and supporting this in our community. ~Angie*

*Karen has a way of teaching us Quiet Leadership through her experiences in
life. So many times I get bored reading books about leadership as most are
not genuine or meaningful. Quiet Leadership is the opposite. Karen shares
her experiences and shows us how we can be better leaders. I laughed so
hard when reading the story of the bears. I had a mentor early in my
professional career. I was just starting as a manager and terrified of him. He
exhibited Quiet Leadership every day and taught me to be a better person
both professionally and personally. This is what Karen has done for all of
us. Thank you for your wisdom and for sharing your experiences. ~Lesleigh
Pagan*

*As a new working mom, reading hasn't been high on my to-do list. Quiet
Leadership changed this. Written in a format that allows you to pick up and
put down, Quiet Leadership has reminded me to take a few minutes every
day for me. And it's been wonderful! Karen, Thank you for the reminder that
when I spend time on myself, not only do my leadership skills grow but my
family and business both thrive and grow as well. ~Genia Castro Waller*

*Through engaging stories, Karen offers the reader practical tools to become
a better leader ...a more effective leader...a quiet leader. In "Quiet
Leadership", Karen's words touch the heart, inspire, and call leaders to
action! ~ Becky Taylor*

This one is dedicated to you. For all you do, and will do to
change your world with a whisper, as a Quiet Leader.
I am glad there is you.

CONTENTS

ACKNOWLEDGMENTS

This book is only possible because each person whose story I told said yes when I asked if I could use it. Names are real names, events are real events, with the blurring lens of time that makes for a good story. I could not do what I do without each of these people and the lesson they taught me. I am grateful, and I hope they know that their Quiet Leadership lesson is being well used, by many people, all trying to be better leaders themselves.

QUIET LEADERSHIP DESCRIBED

I have spent over 25 years watching people grow into leaders and leaders grow into themselves, and I always love the moment when this happens: when the leader grows quiet, their followers lean in, and careful, quiet wisdom finds its way into the room.

I have never been one to lead a riot. That kind of noise can be effective, but in my heart I feel it is not in the cacophony of a riot, but in the stillness of real conversation, in the small spaces left for silence, that leadership grasps hold, movements develop, and changes catalyze.

Give me peaceful, almost whispered moments, and I am all ears. I can hear a leader's heart when they whisper, when they speak their quiet wisdom. And I can feel the tides turn as they speak a truth so loud it can only be heard if you want to hear it.

Quiet Leadership.

Like everything I write, this book is meant to be simple, easily digestible, and enjoyed by opening it to random stories, not necessarily reading from cover to cover. I don't want to overwhelm you with words; instead, I hope you'll be inspired by insights and possibilities.

THINKING ABOUT QUIET LEADERSHIP

Think of the times when you have leaned in, then sat back, satisfied, yet ignited and thinking new thoughts. Think of times when the speaker touched your heart and changed your life.

It was pure.
It was peaceful.
It was awe-inspiring.
It was life-affirming.
It was quiet.
But it changed everything.
Those moments are Quiet Leadership.

Do you recognize the moments Quiet Leadership has worked in your world? When you leaned in to hear a quiet lesson, or when you sat back and realized Dad was right after all? Quiet Leadership is about those moments when you heard wisdom you could apply to your life and your roles, especially your role as a leader. The moments generally sneak up on you, and you almost miss them if you are not open to listening. Life can be like that, throwing out the lessons while you are too involved in living the moment to catch the wisdom tossed your way.

The best Quiet Leaders stop from time to time to reflect and embrace the lessons they are learning. They hold onto the best, most usable lessons, and let the rest slide away. As I have grown as a Quiet Leader, and watched others do the same, it is apparent that the lessons that most often stick are the ones learned quietly, from people who aren't necessarily leading the pack, but instead, influencing the world with their own deep wisdom of how the world works.

As this book has come together, as I've shared the lessons, I find it is easiest to help you grow if I break them into three main leadership categories. That way you are more likely to catch the lesson, because you are looking for it in your work and life, wherever you need it at the time.

The first category is that of a Quiet Leader; you must understand yourself. You can't lead if you don't know who you are, why you are doing the things you do, or the ways in which you need to adjust your own personal sails. These lessons are just for you, opportunities to think about who you want to be as a person and a leader. The lessons will serve you as a leader no matter your role, but I hope they also sit in your heart and help you be just a little more you, to let you trust yourself, and your unique wisdom as a Quiet Leader.

Secondly, there is leading a team. This is the obvious work of leaders and what most of us want to improve at doing. To be an effective leader takes both consistency and the ability to flex with the situation. The lessons in this section will have the most result on your outcome if you listen to them. Leading others is one of the most significant challenges you can take on, and it has the most rewards. When your people "get it"—when they accomplish the task, achieve the goal, help you fulfill the mission—that, my friend, is the most satisfying moment in leadership. I hope you have many of them, both quietly and with cheers so loud they fill your soul.

Thirdly, I'll help you to take community action. We are at a point in our society where we are looking for leaders, people who know a better way or can at least see through the fog and show us the way to tomorrow. While anyone can sound the foghorn to get attention, I want you to imagine yourself and your people, the people you will gather, all focused on moving in in the same direction. Efficiently, quietly moving forward towards a better outcome. Think of the changes you can make. I finally found my true self when I led my first community project; I discovered what it meant to have a voice, demand a change, and see the result, a result that mattered. Asking a community to follow you is different than a work team; it is an army of volunteers, and it can be heady and scary. And you can do it with quiet strength.

Like everything I write, this book is meant to be simple, easily digestible, and enjoyed by opening it to random stories, not necessarily reading from cover to cover. I don't want to overwhelm you with words; instead, I hope you'll be inspired by insights and possibilities.

When I read, I often ask the universe for the words I need and then open the book to a random page, always finding just what my soul needs. If that happens to you because of these pages, I will feel like I have done my work as an author and as a Quiet Leader.

To be a Quiet Leader is to stand tall, help others, and do it in such a manner that you gather people who want to help you change the world, or at least your little corner of it. It is to show up for right, support the quest for better, no matter what better looks like, and it is to say no when wrong is wrong.

SILENCE

For me, some places don't just inspire me with silence; they seem to inflict it into my life, my very being. When I first visited the Redwoods in California, it was one of those places. As I got out of the rental car, rain dripping down the collar of my jacket, I could not utter a word. I could only stand in respectful silence as I touched their ancient bark, as I marveled at their majestic height. There were no words, but there were a few tears as I felt my soul expand to encompass their grandeur. The silence that wrapped my heart was as thick as an ancient woolen quilt: sturdy, comfortable, complete.

I felt the same silence the first time I stepped into the Caribbean Sea, a place so warm, so achingly beautiful, so clearly a place to savor, that all I could do was absorb the rhythmic gift of the waves as I stood in the surf. Silently.

Fireworks—loud, pounding, reverberating fireworks—do the same thing for me, rendering me speechless as I absorb their drama and the act of teamwork that made their ever so brief burst of color in a night sky possible. How can an "ohhhhh" or an "aww" explain what their power does to my heart? It can't, so I watch, silently.

And then, dear reader, there is Mount Rushmore. Strong. Steady. Silent. A granite tribute to teamwork, dreams, and change. I grew up, I like to say, in its shadow, under the noses of the greats, in Custer, South Dakota. Mount Rushmore inspired me with its steady, rock-solid devotion to ideals, ideals big enough to found a nation and guide it into a future that could not be imagined from the back of a horse, in a house without central air.

While I no longer live near this monument, I visit it each time I am home. Each time I visit, I find myself amazed, almost speechless, as I ponder what the leadership of those presidents and their followers, mentors, detractors, and even adversaries meant to my life, my country, and my vision of leadership.

These men lived and died passionate about their convictions, values, and dreams. They fought long, brutal, fiery battles not just to preserve, but to shape the future of a tiny country that would grow into a world power. They carefully stated how a country should be run, a society built, in their opinion. They were chosen to be part of this memorial in tribute to their efforts.

I doubt the same will ever happen for you or me, that our likeness will be captured in stone, our words drilled into the minds of schoolchildren. I doubt that they imagined this for themselves either. Yet here they are, quietly, stoically, with steadfast glares, displaying the strength of Quiet Leadership.

Did they lead as I would? No. Did they behave in ways that would never fly today? Yes. Would they understand the way we look at the world now? No. Do they still have something to teach us? Yes, I think they do. There are several lessons a Quiet Leader can take away from these stone-faced men.

Give everything you have to give. Everything. Your time, your talent, your money, your home, your deepest, most essential values. You need to put them all out there.

Stand firm. When you know that right is right, wrong is wrong, and that compromise won't do, don't waver. Be the lone voice in the wilderness if you must, but stand firm.

Loyalty matters. Being loyal to a person and your relationship with them will win more battles, more elections, more true friends, and ardent followers than you will win by being wishy-washy, in it for yourself, or an ego-fueled leader.

Patience. Building anything remarkable does not happen overnight. Change takes time. No matter what you are trying to do, it will take a lot of doing and a lot of waiting. If what you are doing, like building a community, is more significant than yourself, there will be a process of order, disorder, and reordering. That happens slowly, with constant tending.

Give in. There are things you know, and then, there are things you can't possibly know or understand. Find people who do, listen to them, trust them, and follow them down the path to compromise. It never hurts to give in, as long as you don't give up.

Quiet Leadership came to me as an idea during the Covid-19 pandemic. There was a lot of yelling in the media, in our homes, even at our holiday tables. There was finger wagging and blame throwing, but sometimes there was also a heroic, vivid, active beauty as we figured out how to care for one another in new ways. I saw people helping people, with actions both large and small, doing whatever they could to care for, to lead, and to help us through the panic and into the calm realizations that a tiny germ was bigger than any of us, or our current knowledge.

As I watched, I strove to find a way to embrace and celebrate that beauty, maybe even influence a quieter, less chaotic way of stewarding significant changes. When I started looking around, I found that Quiet Leadership was and is everywhere. As in the examples I have given here, Quiet Leadership is as old as time; it is in oceans and ancient forests, dark skies lit by the fireworks we have been working to perfect for centuries, and it is in old men building a new nation whose likeness were carved into stone. It is also in the voices raised to stop injustice and of those serving the ill from behind a mask.

To be a Quiet Leader is to stand tall, help others, and do it in such a manner that you gather people who want to help you change the world, or at least your little corner of it. It is to show up for right, support the quest for better, no matter what better looks like, and it is to say no when wrong is wrong. Quiet Leadership is quietly saying thank you to those who serve beside and behind you, never forgetting that you can make a difference worthy of a memorial, even if you started out penniless in a log cabin.

Imagine yourself standing in a place that impacts you with its silence. What does it teach you? What can you take away and offer the world? The silence of the Redwoods, the persistence of the ocean, the stoic strength of faces in stone, they all have something to teach us. Quiet Leader, your wisdom comes from these silent places, from these people. All you have to do is listen, and know.

PART ONE   QUIETLY LEADING YOURSELF

Being your authentic self is the most significant gift you can give to yourself and the world. Enjoy being you. Quietly.

It is in knowing ourselves that we gain knowledge of others. It is in understanding what makes us tick, what makes us fume, and what makes us calm and comfortable that makes us better leaders, with the ability to lead from beside and behind, with praise and not an iron fist.

Quiet Leaders take time to think about their journey, to understand why they are on this path, what makes it hard, what makes it breathtakingly beautiful. Quiet Leaders dedicate as much time to caring for and growing themselves as they do applying care and feeding to the rest of their team. This can be done in a myriad of ways, and care of yourself as a leader should be sacred on your calendar. I didn't always practice this. I was too busy going places, getting things done, impressing my people, and searching for the next project to stop and think about who I was and why I was doing the things I was doing. Then I crashed, which wasn't pretty.

After the crash, I began to practice these four things:

Find Me Time. Me Time is not pedicures and self-care; maintenance is not enough for Me Time. Weekly Me Time is dedicated time to read, reflect, or learn. I have time blocked out on my calendar, in red, and I only allow others to crash into that time if the experience makes me a better leader and I will learn something from the person I am allowing into that time slot. I have to admire them, have a quest for what they offer, or they don't get the slot. Often this slot is used for long walks in the woods, where I have time to think. Other times it is sitting in a class or learning a new physical skill. The idea is to walk out of Me Time with a sense of worth, wonder, and contentment.

Block out nonworking hours. It is not fair to yourself, your family, or your tribe if you never take a break. As an entrepreneur or a leader, especially when you're in start-up or crisis mode, it is easy to work all hours of the day and night. It is easy to speak only of your tasks, and demand others leave you alone while working, and cancel your attendance at events that could get in the way of progress. This is the wrong approach that can be fixed by first establishing when you *don't* work. I suggest you *don't* work for at least an hour after getting home at the end of the day. You don't even think about work from 9:00 p.m. to 7:00 a.m. You don't work during dinner. You don't work during car rides with your family, and you don't work on Sunday (or another day of the week), and you sure as hell don't work when someone you love is crying. Once you come up with the hours you are not working, you can post those hours as a signal of focus to you and those who may interrupt your day. Post both the times that you are not working and the times that you are. This clarity leads to increased effectiveness (you *must* get the project done before teatime with the girl in the princess dress at four o'clock), and you can focus on the task at hand when you know you will focus on your people later. It also eliminates the whine ("You're always working.")

Define a Life Mission. *My mission is to use my creativity and positivity to help teams and individuals achieve their Nexts.* If the work, the project, or the client do not fit my mission, I can politely say no. I know what I am trying to do, why I am trying to do it, and what I am good at doing. I also know that I do my very best work when mission-focused, and I have a blast doing it. It takes a moment to clarify your mission, and by moment I mean it can take years, but once you know it, you know it. I like simple missions that reflect your values and give you a vision for what you want to accomplish. It is out of the scope of this book to help you write your mission statement, but a skilled coach or a wise mentor can help you do just that. Again, understand yourself; it makes you authentic, happier, and gives you a feeling of contentment, as you lead others.

ASK FOR HELP. Let me say that again. Ask for help. *Ask for help.* ASK FOR HELP! You cannot do it all, nor should you. If you don't like doing something, hire it done. If you aren't doing your work because of undone projects nagging at you, ask someone to help you. Hire a life or business coach, or work with a mentor—one you will genuinely listen to; the clarity will improve your results. Cleaning toilets—not for you. Changing the oil—why? You should be focused on your personal mission and the mission of the work you are doing for the world. When you ask for help, that is what you get to do: the right work. The argument I hear most often is, "I can't afford help," to which I say, "Bullshit." If you are doing the right work, you are making money (and if you are not, we need to talk), so while someone is being paid to help you, your focus should be on making ten times their cost in sales or income.

There is another reason to ask for help, one that fits right in with being a Quiet Leader: asking for help is a gift you give to another. You are doing the work of a leader; you are taking the punches, making the hard decisions, and tossing the glitter. Some people would never want to do the job you are doing in their wildest dreams. But—and this is the beauty of the world—they would like to do the work you don't want to do. It is a gift to them when you let them do it. Everyone likes to be helpful. Everyone likes to contribute. Everyone likes to give whatever they have to provide the world. Let them. It is the kindest, quietest gift you can give them. Let people help, and both of you will grow because of that act.

You are the kind of person I admire, the kind of person I love to work with and for. I know this because you are still reading, still thinking about something that interests us both: being a better leader. I also know this because I have taken the time to think about and refine who I am as a human and a leader, which is what I am prescribing to you. Think about who and what you want to be, then be that.

Being your authentic self is the most significant gift you can give to yourself and the world. Enjoy being you. Quietly.

Quiet Leaders often let others take the praise and raise their people in front of the cheering crowds instead of demanding credit for themselves. To a Quiet Leader, receiving recognition is less critical than bestowing recognition.

My story does not include formal education. For a long time, that was because I didn't think I was worthy of one; I honestly didn't even understand how to go to college, so that didn't help me overcome a teacher telling me I was too stupid to attend college. Later, there simply wasn't time. Now, well, now I am a bit bullheaded, and when I think, *Gosh and golly, I should get a degree*, I follow that with the bullheadedness of my family and think, *No way, I've come this far, I'll show what I can accomplish without one, by damn*. Perhaps it is flawed thinking, but it keeps me dedicated to continually learning more from so many people and places that sometimes I forget how far I have come. Hard work trumps big brains, sometimes.

When we moved to Alaska, we found that muscles earned more than brains in that frontier setting. My husband, Paul, dove into construction work, and I dove into sales and entrepreneurship. My entrepreneurship started with a cleaning business for new-construction homes. I learned many lessons while cleaning houses, like meeting expectations and exceeding them, organization, the importance of process, and that even when I think it is all about me, it is rarely all about me. I learned that lesson the day I was cleaning windows on a high-profile home carpeted with snowy white wool carpets. The razor blade I was using slipped and cut the base of my thumb, blood spurted, and I went into drama mode. As I whimpered, every single person on the job—the plumber, the painter, a laborer, my husband, and whoever else was around—screamed in unison, "Get off the carpet!" I was a bit shell-shocked. Would no one bring me a Band-Aid? Did no one care that *I* was in pain? Eventually, the answer was yes, but only if *I* was smart enough to save the expensive carpet.

That turned out to be a pivotal day for me. I realized I wanted more. Now, a brilliant woman would have hired employees, franchised a cleaning business, and made more with a team of helpers, but I went into daycare. I figured I could still take my daughter to work, but I wouldn't face ladders and razor blades as part of my daily routine in daycare. I quickly moved from classroom aid to assistant director, stepping over people who had worked there longer than me because I took on the extra tasks, attended all offered training events, and figured out what the business needed to flourish, while the lead teachers figured out what the kids needed, which was their gift, not mine. I was developing a nose for leadership.

Leaving daycare, I moved from one Next to another. I learned everything I could and worked as hard as a mule every chance I got, no matter what my roles were. I showed up early, took on the extra chores, and quietly made myself indispensable. I offered ideas, worked out details, and was enthusiastic when others on the teams I worked with were simply along for the ride, often saying things like *That's not my job,* or *I don't get paid to do anything besides this, and that is all I am going to do.*

When I worked at a national corporation, everyone worked hard. We were on the go, growing at a rapid pace, figuring out as we went along how to help others achieve their goals. It was my dream job, and every day I would work until I couldn't work anymore. During one project, I would get up at 2:30 a.m., work for several hours while my inbox was quiet, shower, and then take on the normal day. Because the company was growing, there was always the opportunity for advancement and challenges that offered experience, if not better pay. I was blessed to be asked to help on exciting projects and to move up more often than some on our team, including a woman with a master's degree.

She was kind, faith-filled, and worked hard for her region but wasn't seen as a team player. Each time I'd get a promotion, she would whine, "But I have the master's degree." Unfortunately she had enough opportunities to repeat that whine that eventually the CEO said, "I know you have a master's degree, but Karen works harder and gets better results." I can't imagine how hard that was for her to hear, as she was working *her* level of hard, but her level of hard was not eye-catching, and it certainly wasn't getting the results I was throwing on the board. Now, I don't say this to sound pompous; I say this because if you look to the right and you look to the left, and people are moving ahead faster than you, you probably need to check your ego and see what you can do to change the landscape. Hard work gets noticed.

You see leaders, at least the best, most respected leaders that I know, quietly and diligently work harder than others in the room, and they get better results. They try one way and then another, without grandstanding. They show up early, say yes to extra tasks and challenges, and they always keep their eye on the stats. They ask themselves daily what they can affect, what can they improve, who on their team needs water, and who needs to be cheered. That's what runs through their minds. What can I do now, what can I do next, and what is our client looking for? They are not looking for accolades, promotions without cause, or credit for a job well done. Those things happen, but usually quietly. No, the leaders who lead by working harder and getting better results let the results speak for themselves, and they smile to themselves when it is clear their efforts are making a difference.

Quiet Leaders often let others take the praise and raise their people in front of the cheering crowds instead of demanding credit for themselves. To a Quiet Leader, receiving recognition is less critical than bestowing recognition.

So if you want to get ahead, if you're going to be seen as the person who deserves to be chosen for the next big project, start now, where you are, working harder and getting better results. Do this because bleeding on the carpet isn't going to get you the attention you desire or deserve, but working hard and getting better results is.

Being scared does not always make sense.

Being scared is also completely human.

Often—and this is a hard truth—being scared is just because we want to be scared.

SCARED TO DEATH

It happens to all of us, those moments when we are so scared to move forward, so afraid of the threat, real or perceived, that the idea of going ahead is so far from comprehension that we stop. We just stop. We don't know how to quiet our heart, button up our courage, or face the fact that this might be the thing that does us in. Sometimes it is because we learned a hard truth. Sometimes it is because what we are being asked to do is bigger than us, beyond our capacity. Sometimes we are embarrassed, we are afraid of being left or having to leave. Sometimes it is the boogeyman, and sometimes it is a situation we walked straight into and can't tell you quite why. We know that inactivity is not the answer, but still, we can't move.

Being scared does not always make sense.

Being scared is also completely human.

Often—and this is a hard truth—being scared is just because we want to be scared.

We don't have all of the info, we don't feel like we have any power, and we sure as hell don't want to face what we have to face because we have not entirely examined what we are facing. That's what Abby reminded me of when she told me her story.

Abby was part of an AmeriCorps volunteer team that stayed with us at Luccock Park during the summer of 2021. (See the later chapter "Kitchen Duty" for more about Luccock Park.) She and her team were full of life, living an adventure while serving America across the west, yet ready to go home. They had been to the city, lived in the mountains, learned things about the world and each other that they never expected to learn. As they sat with us, around campfires and under the trees, I began to understand that the lessons they were learning would serve them well. That the pain they endured would come back later as wisdom, and the knowledge would offer them a perspective few others know.

Still, when you are 18–20, living away from home for the first time, and under a constant budget crunch, it is perfectly normal to say, "I would never do this again." When you toss in a bruin as a camp visitor, it is customary to talk about the time you were most scared, which Abby did.

From Massachusetts, she went on an adventure with a friend in California. They set out for a hike, and Abby, who seems at all times both thought-filled and enthusiastic about life, was concerned for her safety, on high alert; bears frequented the area. When she made it around a bend and looked out across the field, Abby saw several brown bears, enough bears that her heart stopped, fear took over, and fight or flight became sit down and accept the worst.

She sat on a stump, facing the bears, and knew she was going to die. In her mind, there was no way to make it out alive, so she would just wait for the end. Now, Abby tells this story with a calm sense of wonder that she is alive to tell it. She paused for a moment, and we thought about her sitting there, so calmly scared to death. Too scared to fight, too scared to cry, waiting for the end.

If you have read *Seasoned: The Husband I Never Knew*, you know that Paul has spent a great deal of time around bears. Bears and their stories are part of our life. I must say, I have never seen anyone so calm about facing their demise at the jaws of a bear, but here was this child, this sweet young woman who volunteered ten months of her life to help others, sitting on a stump calmly facing the end.

That is when her friend walked back to see what was taking so long. When she saw Abby, just rocking back and forth on the stump, she said, "Abby, what's up?" Abby whispered and pointed towards the field, "bears." Her friend looked at her and quietly said, "Abby, those are just cows."

Abby quickly got up and started walking forward, over the fear, laughing at herself, and pretty damn glad that really wasn't the end.

And that, dear reader, is what I want to leave you with at this point, that fact that whatever you are facing, whatever you are scared to death of is probably not the end. The thing you are most scared of right now is probably not even a bear. Even though it has all of the signs of ending your life, it is probably just a cow, and it is probably going to let you pass, let you live your life to help others, with nary a moo or a swish of its tail.

Seldom is leadership found in might makes right, or flawlessly repeating a lesson from a leadership guru. I have witnessed that the strongest leaders have risen when the team relinquishes hierarchical power and gives into relational, creative, collaboration.

COLLECTING SILENCE

It was 1:30 a.m., somewhere on the Alaska Canadian Highway in the Yukon Territory. It was also 30 degrees below zero, and I was traveling with my husband, Paul, and our six-year-old daughter, Liz. The centerline of the highway, which was just a frozen strip across the tundra, had parallel white lines running on either side of it. For miles, we had wondered what they were, why they were running perfectly down the center of the road, and not to either side, in a line as tire tracks would be. Then, coming around a blind corner, a semi-truck with lights ablaze nearly ran us off the road. Straddling the center line was standard practice on icy northern roads, we learned in a coffee shop later. Driving down the center of the road provided the driver with increased reaction time if a moose or buffalo appeared in the headlights, That may be true, but it didn't really provide us with maneuverability on that tight corner. Once we understood the system, we settled into speeding through the night in a place without other humans by straddling the yellow line, trusting those white lines to keep us out of ditches, off of cliffs, and prevent meeting a moose nose to grill.

Later, as we came down a mountain pass, awed by how the moonlight danced across the field of snow, flitting in and out of the tree line, which eventually swallowed the light, we saw them, the northern lights. It wasn't the first time we had seen them; we'd been living in Anchorage, Alaska, for several years, and northern lights often danced above the city late at night or early in the morning. We always stopped to watch them, easily mesmerized by the colors, the movement of the auroral ribbons flowing across a dark sky. These were different, though.

They were bigger, brighter, spread across the entire horizon, uninterrupted by ambient light, with miles of the crystalline valley to call home. They were ethereal, dramatic enough that we had to stop, climb into our snow gear, and get out and enjoy them. We turned off the pickup and lay on the warm hood without speaking, unwilling to spoil the magic with mere words that could never do this cosmic show justice. It was our daughter who eventually pointed out that they were making noise. Beautiful, quiet, electric snapping as they went whizzing across the silent sky, with a peaceful yet exuberant crackling. We'd read the stories of Klondikers who reported these phenomena, but we'd also read it wasn't true, that science couldn't back the claims of auroral whispers.

But there we were, in a place of absolute silence, unfettered by wind or the noisy detritus of human drama, listening to one of the most beautiful sounds I'd ever heard. I knew I was hearing it only because of the silence. Silence so thick you could almost touch it. I'd never heard silence like that before, and now, when I think of that night, my nose seems to get cold, my heart seems to calm, and I feel the peace we felt that night—utter and complete peace. The kind of peace that makes you believe in a Christmas Star, of holy nights and the great beyond. It was as if the entire galaxy was laid out there before us, every star, every bit of deep space telling us its secrets.

We stayed, cuddled on that pickup hood, until the metal that had given us every molecule of warmth caused us to shiver. Reluctantly we crawled back inside the now 30-below cab and, with colossal dread, started the engine that earlier, while we were straddling the yellow line, felt powerful and comforting but now felt like the most significant disturbance we had ever known.

With a turn of the key, the silence broke.

Noise has always been part of my human experience. As a child, even when I escaped a house with a cacophony of children's voices, the day was punctuated with trains, noon whistles, and the whisper that often sounds like a roar of wind through pine needles. When I was a child, my mom kept the TV on all day for company, and when I was a young bride, my husband wanted to fall asleep to the sounds of his childhood, a radio tuned to a distant city. There were hammers and saws, pets and people, work and games, frivolity and chatter—always, always some sort of noise to play as background music to my life.

Until that night, that magical, once-in-a-lifetime night that defies an apt description, no matter how hard I try. It was a silent, crackling night.

I think it was then that I began not only to crave silence but to carve it out in my life. I turned off the TV, the radio, the constant stream of people through my house. I sat under trees in the woods, meditated while watching a beaver play in a mountain pond, and wore earplugs to sleep in hotels or while traveling on a plane. Quiet space, I found, did not need to be filled with noise, and this was something of a surprise to me. There was beauty in silence, listening to the hum of nothing but blood crawling quickly through my veins.

I became whole while listening to the sound of nothing but air.

And then, as if a gift of divine disturbance, I was given the idea for Canvas Creek Team Building, the idea to ask groups of people to create art together, in silence, a seemingly impossible task that over 80,000 people have successfully accomplished.

While standing behind and beside them, I have witnessed the gifts we can give one another in silence. I have learned to look for the nods, the flinches, the vibrant canvas collecting brushstrokes, and the unmitigated joy of a tiny addition applied by the timidest of the group. I have seen tears, heard laughter, and discovered that when people finally look into themselves while trusting the group to help carry them along, they smile sweetly and grow in confidence and stature.

It is beautiful.

And it is silent. Or at least kind of silent.

Canvas Creek almost always involves music because I can influence the pace of the experience with the beat of a drum, but it seldom involves verbal communication. At the last moment, after hearing the other rules, teams are told that they will paint in silence. There are gasps, laughs, and a few "holy shits" when I give this direction, and then, almost amazingly, the team begins to paint, side by side, but individually at first. They vie for space or try to lead the process towards the outcome they alone desire until the pull of collaboration is stronger than the desire to dominate. When that happens, everything changes.

They "hear" one another, even though they aren't saying anything.

People without a voice in the boardroom suddenly speak up in color and movement. People who can't for the life of them shut their traps fill in every white space on the canvas with bold and dynamic color, and the rest of the team lets them. People who feel shut out and unimportant in daily decisions let their opinion be heard by overlaying with paint their vision on someone else's art. In a matter of minutes, the team goes through everything you have come to expect from a team that is growing together; there is storming, norming, and forming. There are tribal dances and swaths of paint across many faces, and there is the oh-so-human journey down the path of order, disorder, reordering that makes tremendous changes possible.

And then, afterward, as they look at their art, whether beautiful or pitiful, they nod their heads, poke each other with their elbows, and they smile. They have created something lovely, meaningful, powerful, something that captures what only they could say, together.

In silence.

It is in standing beside and behind these teams that I grew the most in my understanding of leadership. Seldom is leadership found in might makes right, or flawlessly repeating a lesson from a leadership guru. I have witnessed that the strongest leaders have risen when the team relinquishes hierarchical power and gives into relational, creative, collaboration. When team members are brave enough to say, I cannot do this alone without uttering a word. When they realize that perfection will be overrated. When, about 13 minutes into the process, they are no longer painting for themselves but for the good of the whole.

Soon they realize that no matter what work they do, what role they fill, what rules govern their path, working for the good of the whole is the only thing that matters, and unbelievably they now realize that is the only thing they want to do both on the canvas and back at the office.

It is in new styles of collaboration, new methods of communicating that wise leaders lean into Quiet Leadership, a leadership that is smooth, collaborative, and patient. It is then that changes happen, processes are improved, and goals are shattered. It is when the team finally, while holding a paintbrush, admits they are somehow a team no matter what, that genuinely effective leadership reigns.

And that leadership, Quiet Leadership, more often than not falls back on the lessons the leader learned from aunts and uncles, neighbors, coaches, or sitting silently under a tree, listening to the universe and its quiet, confident hum. These subtle, everyday lessons, developed through life experiences and quiet observation, form the underpinning of the strongest leader's character.

I am in awe of silence now. I collect it, protect it, and always try to share it with others. Just like these stories, and those that will follow once this book is published, I feel the need to collect, protect, and share them because these, the quiet lessons of leadership, seem to be the ones with the most power. The ones that, if you listen, as we did that night in the Yukon Territory, thrum with a truth you can't mistake.

You don't have to launch the grenade to make changes, but you can't run when it's tossed either.

STRONG AS A TANK

I have never laughed so hard in my life as when sitting beside a man called Tank. He knows exactly what to say, what accent to say it in, and just how loud to say it to make me break into uncontrollable, tear-streaming, bladder-clenching laughter. He also knows how to make me cry while feeling hope for abused children in our world.

As Frank Warren of PostSecret once told me, sometimes the children who are the most damaged by the world grow up to do the most good for the world.

That sums up Tank. Tank was raised by a mom who is a district judge for the Montana Supreme Court, and a dad who made one too many bad decisions, eventually telling his boys, at gunpoint, that he didn't want anything to do with them. Tank, whose real name is Remington, retreated into a pit of sadness and the heavy duty of protecting his mom and brother at all hours while still trying to grow into a teen. It was during that time that a Rotarian decided to send Tank to RYLA (Rotary Youth Leader Awards). At RYLA, after four days of silence, of trying to hide in the corner, Remington finally told someone his story.

As soon as he opened up, the team I facilitate RYLA with, and I decided to raise him into a man and invite him back year after year, because his heart deserved our love, and his fervor to protect and grow others had leadership written all over it. At the beginning of year two, Remington, who weighed over 300 pounds, but carried the heart of a purring kitten, ran across the meadow at full tilt. He was faster than anyone else on the team, including many track stars and other athletes without the girth. Of course, they were also without the desire Remington had to get away from the spider his mentor, whom he calls Papa Paul, was threatening to throw at him.

The rumble of those thundering feet still rings in my heart. So do the tears I have seen RYLA campers shed when they open up and tell this bull of a man their deepest, scariest secrets.

Tank was a nickname lovingly given to this soul, a name that summed up the power of his movements and the strength of his convictions. From a young age, Tank knew, deep down, without a doubt, that he was playing the long game when it came to protecting children, that this was his destiny. His mom helped him understand the law, and his dad helped him know why laws need to be upheld, so Tank began training his mind and body to be strong.

Weightlifting, studying, more weightlifting, mentoring RYLA attendees with wisdom and humor, Tank grew from a scared boy to a man headed to law school so that he could defend abused children from their assailants.

Tank does all of this quietly, stoically, with the kind of warmth that draws you in and the kind of power that makes you feel like the world, or at least those in his world, are going to be just fine in the end. And that is what I have learned from Tank, time and again, that when it matters, when it truly, deep in your gut matters, it is best to stand like a tank, unmovable, with a quiet strength that transforms the battle as soon as the engine starts to rumble. You don't have to launch the grenade to make changes, but you can't run when it's tossed either.

Stand still. Feel your fervor. Be Strong as a Tank.

Quiet Leadership

Sometimes you are the only one who can see the end goal, understand that the sacrifices are worth it, that what you are doing, what you believe in, can only be lived by you.

YOU STAND ALONE

I think the best leaders have all had times when they stand alone, when what they are doing is a little too much, a little too scary, or simply has not caught on yet. They hold on to their convictions, goals, and cause, because they know it is the right thing for them, and in doing so, they allow others the grace to follow, watch, or ignore as they wish.

It can be tough to stand alone, but friend, it can also be full of growth.

I am thinking about this today as my grandson Ezra watches us all eat cookies while he has nothing.

It's not an allergy, an illness, or a punishment; it is pure willpower, willpower that I am sure will take him a long way in this world. When Ezra was four, Pampa (Paul) taught him how to control his mind so that when someone tickled him, he wouldn't laugh. If Ezra saw you coming with fingers posed for tickling, he would take a deep breath, endure the frantic vibrations, and then give you a very stoic, satisfied grin. He'd thwarted your efforts to make him lose control.

When he was 11, I told him about a young man, Luke, who had gone sugar-free for a year and been rewarded with $250 by his parents. They were sure they'd saved way more than $250 on sugary drinks. Of his own volition, Ezra said he'd like to try that, so he set a date, January 1, as that's a good date to start a year-long goal, and took off like a shot.

Zero, and I mean zero sugar passed Ezra's lips. He read labels, turned down birthday cake and soda treats, and, as only a human with solid willpower can do, ended each day with a sense of accomplishment over weakness. Along the way, he inspired some of his friends to try the sugar-free life, telling them how much better he felt, but they would soon drop off because most of them were missing what Ezra had in mind: a big goal.

Ezra quickly turned the idea of $250 into a request for a $600 animation tablet, to which I said, "Sure!" as I had a feeling he'd be back on sugar at the next party. He was not. He went six months, took a break because, in the Covid world, it seemed like a few treats were in order, and then, on January 1, 2021, he started in again, with a new dedication to his goal.

We are eight months in now and, except for a bite or two of dessert while on vacation, he is sugar-free; 12 years old and sugar-free. That is impressive, isn't it!

There are so many leadership lessons here—vision, goals, conviction—but the one that rings loudest to me as I watch him quietly stand by as others indulge is that leadership is often lonely. Sometimes you are the only one who can see the end goal, understand that the sacrifices are worth it, that what you are doing, what you believe in, can only be lived by you. No matter how many people follow you, in those moments when you stand alone, you have influence and your resolute devotion gives encouragement to others who, as you do, stand alone.

Goal getting is like ride getting; you have to be interesting, and by that I mean be a bit of a character about your goal. Let people know what it means to you, laugh about it, shout about it, have fun sharing it. Most importantly, put significant effort into it getting it. When you are moving forward, others will want to help you get there.

Have you ever put your thumb out and hoped for a ride? Are you the type of person who picks up hitchhikers? Do you see hitchhiking as an interesting, hopeful way to move about, or as a scary annoyance, possibly a person hell-bent on death and mayhem, if only you pull over?

I grew up in a town, an area really, filled with tourists. Some arrived by car, some by bus, and some—the most interesting ones—by thumb. We were taught not to talk to them, not to give them a ride, but not really to be afraid of them either. They were just humans going about their business while we went about ours. That is why, when my Mom whipped the car to the side of the road to pick up a hitchhiker, I was totally shocked.

Mom had a car full of kids, all bouncing around from front to back and back again. The youngest was in a car seat that was not actually a seat but a strap system that allowed her to sit, stand, turn around, and nap without interrupting the driver. It also didn't limit much of her freedom. As you can probably guess, this was a time before seatbelt laws, back when my Aunt Francis summed up the strap system by saying, "Why are you restraining that poor child? She will hate riding in a car if you do that." To say picking up a hitchhiker was out of character for Mom is spot-on accurate. Mom didn't have time for frivolity, patience for trouble, or space for baggage.

It turns out, however, the person she picked up was no ordinary hitchhiker; it was none other than Mary Two Eagles, a local celebrity and friend to all. Mary had a pack on her back, a back that was permanently curved towards the ground, but her nose was pointed forward. I don't know all of Mary's story; I'm not sure anyone does, but I've pieced together that she loved hamburgers, and if she knew you and she smelled burger cooking for dinner, she would just open the door, sit at the table, and have dinner without waiting for an invite. No one ever said no, because she was a kind soul with a hard life. I recently learned that Mary was a white woman who married a Native American before these things were part of the norm, in a town where that was just fine, but it didn't make work any easier to find, or life any easier to live. When her beloved husband died, she looked to the fridge, looked around the cabin, and realized she didn't have much to her name except a horse, a Chihuahua, and a spectacular Indian chief headdress, which she had often worn while standing beside her spouse.

So, knowing she didn't have a lot of options besides the grace of living in a western tourist town, Mary put on that headdress, set her dog on her lap, and rode into town. She sat on the corner, patiently, quietly, waiting for someone to take her photo, and boy howdy did they. People would make U-turns in the middle of the street, exclaiming excitedly at her appearance and jumping out of the car, asking for a photo. They would often have polite conversations with her, which were probably pretty short because Mary was a woman of few but well-chosen words, as I recall.

Sometimes, however, they would take the photo and turn without giving her a dollar or even a quarter, and little tiny Mary, who was no bigger than a sprite and sat silently, hunched over on her horse, would slide off that horse faster than you can say cheapskate and chase after the offender with a wild demand for justice. It was blood-curdling for them, but it was great fun for us kids to watch. The tourist would quickly hand her the money and dash to the safety of their car or the into next store on the block. I imagine that to this day, some of those tourists still tell the story of being chased by Mary during their Wild West adventure! They probably leave out the part of trying to cheat a little old lady, sitting on a horse, with a Chihuahua and a bent back, out of a quarter.

So, there we were, driving down the road with a woman who was both a hitchhiker and a local celebrity! We were awestruck, quietly listening to our mom, Mary, and Mary Two Eagles, chatting about the weather. Mary soon got up on her knees and poked her head into the back seat. She said, "Do you kids want to learn how to hitchhike?" "Yes!" was our enthusiastic reply. Mom said, "NO!" but Mary went on, giving us a life lesson.

In her quiet voice that we had to strain to hear as we elbowed our way towards the front seat, she said, "Now, first and foremost, you never ever want to hitchhike with your right thumb. When you use your right thumb, its' because you are just standing there, looking at traffic, hoping they will stop and take you where you are going. If you use your left thumb, it means you are trying to get somewhere, and you will get there with or without their help." (Imagine here, little tiny Mary, bent forward by time, carrying a pack, walking beside the road with her left thumb out and her nose pointed forward.) She said, "You are moving towards your destination, and as they pass you by, they just naturally want to assist you because they see how determined you are to get where you are going."

Now, as you can imagine, this was eye-opening news to a car full of kids who had never been this close to someone with this much life story before. I don't recall what questions we asked, but I remember animated talking until Mary turned and sat, as she did on her horse, quiet and stoic. When we got to the big city, mom bought everyone burgers, Mary included, before she went on her way, bent forward, with the pack on her curved back.

Much to my mom's relief, none of us kids took up hitchhiking. Still, when I started helping individuals and teams shape their goals and define their strategic plans, I observed something significant. The people who let others know where they were going, who shared their goals, objectives, and determination to figure it out, often reached their goals faster than those who just waited, hoping someone would help them. Often, in these sessions, people will share their dream, and someone across the room or sitting quietly in the back will say, "I can help you with that." And that is the absolute beauty of sharing your goals: that someone will know a guy, know a way, or be willing to lend a hand.

The successful individuals put the proverbial left thumb out and move towards their goal while letting others offer assistance.

Goal getting is like ride getting; you have to be interesting, and by that I mean be a bit of a character about your goal. Let people know what it means to you, laugh about it, shout about it, have fun sharing it. Most importantly, put significant effort into getting it. When you are moving forward, others will want to help you get there.

As a leader, especially a quiet one, there is power in sharing your goals, your vision. There is even more power in letting others know what kind of help you need, but—and this is important—letting them know you are going to get there, even if you have to walk all the way yourself. You are that determined. When you show this forward commitment, with your pack strapped to your back and your face bent to the wind, people will naturally want to pitch in and help.

I wish I had gotten to know Mary just a little more, and I wish I could give her a dollar, or a hundred, for every person she has helped achieve their goals, all because she taught a bunch of seat-jumping kids how to hitchhike.

Quiet Leadership

What I want you to know, if you tend more towards bold than timid, more towards pushing than pulling, more towards grumpy than giggly, is that if, like Allen, you are these things yet your heart is kind, and you are willing to throw in a punch line as often as a punch, you too can be a Quiet Leader.

SPREADING HATE AND DISCONTENT

When my daughter, Liz, was seven years old, I heard her planning a surprise birthday party for me. She was calling her friends and my husband Paul's friends, but she wasn't calling my friends. I didn't have any to call. I remember that day vividly. It was late afternoon, and I was sitting in the bathtub, soaking away cramps and a bad attitude. I was also crying as I heard her trying so hard to do something incredibly sweet for me, but knowing that I simply was not interesting enough, known enough, or loved enough for people to drop what they were doing and come to a surprise party the next day. I thought of my fear, that no one would come to my funeral, that my family would sit in an empty church memorializing a woman with no legacy, Liz's calls proved to me that fear had a founding.

I knew, soaking there, that I wasn't who or what I wanted to be, a shy and depressed woman living with too much weight, too much regret, and too little self-worth.

I wanted to be what I learned about when I met Paul and his family: cheerful, upbeat, full of optimism. Paul's dad preached—with a voice that frankly sounded pretty grumpy—to have a positive mental attitude, to look on the bright side, to be the biggest smile in the room. I knew, soaking there, turning into a sad and lumpy prune, that I wanted freedom from my demons. I wanted friends. I wanted to be happy in my skin.

And, so, with years of work, that is what I became. I had to fake it at first, I had to pretend to be happy with myself, I had to pretend to be interesting, I had to pretend to be smart enough to get the jobs I could learn from and to hang with the people who would quietly mentor me as I became, well, me.

And, as I talk about in my book *What's Next,* I faked it until I made it real.

I started with what for me was the mind-blowing idea of fake it till you make it, but I discovered that breeds imposter syndrome. So I learned to fake it until I made it real, and I wasn't faking it anymore. Whatever it is that you are trying to achieve, you can fake it until you make it real.

Faking happiness was a lot of work, and sometimes I still have to catch myself before the doldrums take over and I perform the work to light the smile, but I am glad to say I am truly happy. And I no longer worry that there will be an empty funeral parlor because God is good; people did come to the party Liz planned, and that led me to believe that a few people just might show up to a surprise party for me, tomorrow, if, you know, there was the promise of good food and wine.

So if I have worked this hard to be happy, to collect people who bring me joy, why is one of my favorite people in the world a man who says, "I'm still spreading hate and discontent," when I ask how he is doing?

Why does my heart erupt in laughter when I see Allen Carter's name on my phone? And the even bigger question is this: why does Allen put up with me? We are different in every way people who live in Montana can be different.

He is a born and bred Montanan, with land homesteaded before Montana was a state; I am a transplant. He is gruff; I am not. His wife is an accomplished horsewoman who rocks the heck out of a buckskin dress; I buy Nordstrom suits and ride a beach cruiser bike resplendent with little birds and a heart on the chassis. He sells guns; I don't shoot. He grows grass-fed beef; I like a nice Alaskan salmon. He has scars from a tussle with a mountain lion; I'd rather not. More than 90 years ago, his family sold the land for the mountain camp I managed, and over the years the relationship between the camp and the Carter family has not always been one of, shall we say, conciliatory agreement.

Which is how our story began.

At the time, I was exuberant, taking on my passion project of running Luccock for three years, putting in long hours, and cajoling others to help in my quest to right the ship. We started with epic amounts of cleaning and massive bonfires full of junk that had accumulated like drifts of snow. My helpers and I hauled truckloads of debris to the dump, used lots of elbow grease, and applied hundreds of gallons of paint. My mantra in the early days at Luccock was "Trash is trash," and there were plenty of times to say it! Occasionally, in the frenetic clean-out, we would find a treasure, like three brand new rolls of barbed wire fencing. We didn't have a use for it, but it was too precious for the garbage pile, so on a whim, I offered it to a man I was often told to steer clear of, Allen Carter.

Allen and the previous manager didn't get along, and even though he spreads hate and discontent, I believe those ill feelings were more her doing than his. Over the years, there were tax issues, annoyances caused by guests, and other aggravations. And while I can't speak for him, I believe he carried a regret that his grandma's legacy of allowing this camp to be created in a treasured meadow was not being acknowledged as it deserved.

So chipper, all-is-sunshine-in-the-world me saw Allen stopped along the road outside of camp. I pulled in beside him and flashed my brightest, win-the-sale, wow-the-audience smile. He wasn't impressed. When I told him who I was, calling him Mr. Carter to show my respect, he said, "I know damn good and well who you are." I quaked a little. Okay, a lot. I told him I had barbed wire and wondered if he could use it.

Now, they say good fences make good neighbors, which is what this story could be about, but while I have lived in the city most of my life, I didn't realize the true power of a fence to make that statement true. As if on cue, Allen softened, and I offered to bring the fencing down to him sometime, and he offered to follow me up the hill and pick it up right then.

As I pulled into the camp drive, I wasn't sure if I brought home a puppy I would want to keep or a rattlesnake with a dose of venom for which I didn't have an antidote.

Allen proved to be neither.

We started talking after he collected the fencing and we have not really stopped since that day.

He has given me sage advice, has done more work for camp than some of my employees, introduced me to his people and his life, and has even shown me a secret grove of trees that I am not supposed to tell you that I saw, so I won't. Allen has made me laugh every single time I have interacted with him, often because he plays the grump pretty darn well, and I am content to let him. I knew we were friends, though, when he asked me to do a favor for him as the best of friends do. He wanted a friend to get married at camp during a time it was slated to be closed. That wedding day was unforgettable, with a helicopter delivering the bride and then a hot-air balloon whisking the happy couple above the meadow.

When an unhappy man came into camp, calling me names I'd never been called before, it was my husband, Paul, who tossed him out of camp, and Allen who promised bodily harm if it happened again. There was a comfort in those words, mainly because sometimes you need a person who seems to have not just the courage to back up his bravado but the steel in his eye that makes hiding a body seem logical if it came to that. Thank goodness it didn't come to that! In the end, the villain realized he was in the wrong, and I went back to being happy-go-lucky. Still, during that episode, Allen's robust, sometimes cynical outlook on life gave me comfort.

If you watch my Monday videos, you know I often campaign against the grumps of the world, rally against the heretics who poke holes in my happiness, and I usually try to change their sullen demeanors with a story and a smile. I have learned from my friendship with Allen that, as I often say, it takes a drunk, a preacher, a teacher, and a clown to make a community. You'll read more about this in the chapter Two Drunks and a Mayor. It also takes a man big enough to stand up for what he believes in.

And that is Allen.

He knows right from wrong, leans into what he believes in, and beats the hell out of what he doesn't. Every person I have met in this valley called Paradise knows who he is. Some don't like him, those who fear him seem to have good reason to, and many others describe him as the salt of the earth, the kind of guy who would quietly give you the shirt off his back.

The deal is, those who aren't fans would describe Allen as loud, possibly brash, with a leadership style that involves more telling than asking. But true to my hypothesis, it is the moments when Allen is quiet that he is doing the work of a man with conviction, confidence, and a heart as big as the valley that has always been his home, and it is done quietly. It is done with humble words, cascading humor, and the knowledge that might does not always make right, but it's a handy tool to have. We have an agreement that I don't tell anyone about the good work he has done for me, and he won't stop doing it. (By the way, Allen, I have a new list if you are reading this.)

Allen has taught me to value, more than ever, a leadership style outside of the norm, to appreciate those who allege that they spread hate and discontent because sometimes they make me laugh while keeping me safe from a world I tend to trust too much.

What I want you to know, if you tend more towards bold than timid, more towards pushing than pulling, more towards grumpy than giggly, is that if, like Allen, you are these things yet your heart is kind, and you are willing to throw in a punch line as often as a punch, you too can be a Quiet Leader—the kind of Quiet Leader who makes friends with enemies, earning their utter respect, and sticks in that enemy's heart because of the fences you mend together. Allen is that friend for me, and I hope you are that kind of friend to another if you are the hate-and-discontent type of leader.

What if every day you asked yourself how you could lead those you love to better outcomes, better experiences, and better versions of themselves?

The late Jerry Traylor, author, speaker and fellow Rotarian, and I did not see eye to eye on a lot of things when it came to raising teen leaders. He was adamant that nicknames were the downfall of civilization, and I am convinced being bestowed a loving nickname helps people to grow into their potential. He believed in an agenda full of lectures; I wanted one full of movement to balance out the dead butt syndrome. Even though we differed about several things, I admire his ability to help people understand their worth in the world.

Jerry could do what I am not good at: see the lone soul who needs a hug. I am better at reading a room's energy and adjusting the agenda to pump it up. Jerry would sit for long hours and listen as hurting and broken souls told him their stories, just so he could tell them they had the power to overcome the pain and the unfair ceilings life had put on them. He did it, like a good Quiet Leader, with a whisper. I hope to do the same with a page full of words or a microphone. I also live my life with fully functioning legs, Jerry did this, and so much more, with the constant, overwhelming pain of cerebral palsy.

Jerry ran multiple marathons, climbed Pike's Peak, and crossed the US, from shore to distant shore, on crutches. I shall never do any of those things, crutches or no. Nor will I live up to his greatness as a role model for overcoming personal limitations. He also had a moment in his signature speech that I, as a speaker, wish I had. Jerry would tell his story, shuffling back and forth across the room, raising one cane in the air to make a point, moving from quiet to raucous, enthralling the audience. When they were totally his, he would talk of his decision to cross the US, by himself, on crutches. He would get quiet and ask the group, "What do you think my friends said to that?" Responses would include *you're crazy, they'd laugh, they'd say no way.* Jerry would stop, look dumbstruck and say, "My friends asked how they could help. I don't know what kind of people you are hanging out with, but you might need better friends."

Every single time I heard Jerry say this, there was a gasp, an audible awakening, a realization that your friends really do make you who you are. It is both your privilege and your obligation to be part of a group that offers help instead of negativity to one another.

This story comes to mind today because a friend mentioned overhearing a senior citizen say to his companion, "I need smarter friends," as he scrolled through his phone. His companion replied, "I think I need to be smarter for my friends."

Imagine, if we, the Quiet Leaders made that a life goal, to be smarter for our friends, our teams, our communities. What if every day you asked yourself how you could lead those you love to better outcomes, better experiences, and better versions of themselves? Think how fun it would be to be in your circle! Think of everything you could accomplish, together!

Kelly Cresswell, executive director of Reach Higher Montana, was discussing this theory with her son recently, that he could be the leader, the one to show his friends how to behave, how to make life choices for himself that improved their lives, and got them closer to their goals. Parents often discuss the tired but oh so true "birds of a feather flock together" adage, and just as often it falls on deaf ears. What I loved about Kelly's approach was the reminder that sometimes we should be smarter for our friends. That when we make good decisions for ourselves, we help others to do the same. We not only stay out of trouble, but we also help them to stay out of trouble as well.

People who believe in serving their communities join service organizations, thus multiplying their efforts. People who write music put the words in our mouths. Teens who are taught how to lead end up changing the world, or at least their small part of it. One of the interesting facts about obesity is that if one person is obese, their entire social circle tends to be overweight, if not obese. We are, as can be proven if you look at anyone's food and exercise journal, the sum total of the things we do every day, and the people we hang out with.

Every single day we get to decide if we will hang with friends who make us smarter. We get to decide if we will be the friend who raises another to their full potential. We, the Quiet Leaders, get to decide if we will quietly do nothing, or quietly do something. I would argue that if we quietly choose to do something, especially to be smarter for those around us, we are being the very best version of us that we can be.

Let's be that. Let's do something.

Let's at least try to be smarter for our friends and followers.

When you are in the doldrums, when the Red Ds have taken over, I hope you will look for the blessings, the things you can learn, and know that someday your Red D will be a part of your story, but not the end of your story.

I woke to my daughter and her husband knocking on the door, telling me a sheriff needed to see me. I assumed that one of our cars was stolen or totaled by a drunk driver, because this had been our biggest trouble so far in life. Both had recently happened, both were annoying, and as I walked down the hallway, I wasn't looking forward to dealing with the details.

As I stepped into the living room, I knew this wasn't about a car. I was immediately cold, and the sheriff's face showed the grim news he was about to deliver. My youngest brother, a treasured member of our little tribe, had committed suicide. All I remember was screaming no, crying hard, and then apologizing to the officer for his having to deliver such hard news.

We spent the night in a puddle on the couch, crying, lost, contacting relatives. To be fair, I didn't contact anyone; my family took that on. All I did was sit; shell-shocked that such a happy man could come to such a tragic end. That night was the first of many occasions when my family rallied around me and gave me strength to get from point A to point B, and I was too grief-stricken to tell them I noticed. All I did was breathe for a very long time, and that is what they let me do.

Life spiraled down from there. A few bad decisions and doubt in what, before that, had been a life without doubt, fear, and more decline, heaped onto my shoulders. I found myself letting life take me for a ride and seldom taking a stand for myself. Instead, I waited for the other shoe to drop while I did the bare minimums to sustain life, business, and relationships. I call this being crushed by Red Ds. Death, Disease, Divorce (not part of my story, thank goodness), Debt, bad Decisions, Debilitating circumstances: the list of Ds can be a very long one, and many of us have more than one D at work in our life right now.

With a lot of hard work and a lot of time, I pulled myself out of that decline, got my feet under me, and as I started to thrive I coached others to do the same. Then Covid chaos hit. My mom died on the day the world shut down for Covid. Instead of mourning her, I found myself mourning all of life, including the changes my business would have to endure, being locked away from friends and family. Add to that the lack of toilet paper in my basement warehouse, as I had been traveling home from her sickbed when that alarm rang, and it was all just sad. I am not sure what was worse, the lack of TP or the fact I was not very good at running the TV remote because previously I'd been too in love with living to do much watching, but now watching was all I had the strength to do.

I was knee-deep in an ice cream container when I realized this could not and would not be my life, that BY DAMN, I would not just survive Covid, but I would use the time to get healthier and to build a more substantial business.

By Damn.

I would write my own story, and I would help others write a better story than the world was handing them. I would not die of kidney failure. I would not wither away into obscurity, having people ask, "Whatever happened to Karen?" By Damn.

Making that decision lit me on fire. I developed and implemented a plan. I created a webinar called By Damn for local businesses, and in May of that year, I delivered it to over 2000 people—all for free—to give people hope in a hopeless situation. I lost 25 pounds. I leaned into learning, and I stopped. That is the one thing Covid chaos gave us: the opportunity to stop. I felt the sunshine on my face and the grass under my feet. Being outside is a healing balm, so I sat under many trees that year while growing forward. Always forward.

There are a few things these dances with the Red Ds have taught me, things I'd like to offer to you if you feel crushed under the weight of defeat.

The sun will rise tomorrow, and it is your duty to greet it. Get up, get out, and sing to the sun. If there is nothing else you can do for the day, stand in the glory of a new beginning, and one day you will fully embrace the day as yours.

Forget tolerance. You have been too tolerant for too long. I am not talking about diversity, that you should tolerate. Stop tolerating poor behavior on your part or the intolerable being done to you by others. Stop tolerating an unmade bed, uncombed hair, and life in sweatpants. If it is not serving your highest self, why are you tolerating it?

Help someone. When you are down, out, sad, and ugly, the last thing you think you have is anything else to give, and I am here to tell you that is part of the death spiral. You have something others need. Give knowledge, give cookies, give a pair of socks to the guy on the corner. When you give, your heart opens ever so much, and you can start to feel the warmth of life, even when grief chills your bones.

Plan something for tomorrow. Plan something for a week from now. Beyond that might seem too much, but with nothing to do, nothing to look forward to, your heart has no reason to beat a little faster. We learned this when we owned our ceramic studio, In Good Glazes. Some people felt hopeless, suicidal, and they painted a mug, or a tiny cat, and waiting to see it come out of the kiln seven days later gave them a reason to live for a few more days. Then they would repeat this cycle, and eventually, with prayer and therapy, their life did not require trips to the studio because they were busy, happily living it.

Let others help you. Others don't even know what to do, and they ask, "How are you?" when it is the dumbest question in the world, but they are sent, these people who stop to notice your pain, to serve you, to help you see the light of life. Let them. Often it helps them as much as it helps you.

When you are in the doldrums, when the Red Ds have taken over, I hope you will look for the blessings, the things you can learn, and know that someday your Red D will be a *part* of your story, but not the *end* of your story.

When my brother died, I thought I would be defined and limited by his death. An angel told me I didn't have to be, and I learned, from her and others, how to comfort someone in grief, which before his death I thought meant baking a casserole and cheerfully saying, "I'm sending prayers."

I am a fuller, happier person because of these journeys with the Big Red D, and you will be too. I promise you that. You just have to get through today and tomorrow too.

This chapter was originally published in Yellowstone Valley Woman *magazine, offered in hope that your Red D's make you stronger as a leader.*

Quiet Leadership

Life is a long and incredible journey, filled with highs and lows, tears and laughter. It is in the knowledge that tomorrow will be different from today that there is the greatest hope, an offering of faith that the best is yet to be.

HERE

There is a moment for everyone when life does not seem to fit right. Goals have crashed, people have moved on, illness has taken over, the reality is not as fun as fantasy, or you have let yourself down again.

Each person has been there, and if this is where you are today, tired, frustrated, lost, sad, mad, scared, wondering how you will get there from this pitiful place called here, you are right where you are supposed to be. You might not find a lot of comfort in that, and that might seem less than motivational, but it is true.

When I was living in one of those times, pretty well pissed at the situation I found myself in, and knowing full well I put myself there, I tried escaping with a long drive by myself. I heard an interview with Toby Keith on the radio, an artist I liked but not someone I would seek out. Toby was riding high at the time, hit after hit, accolades and money rolling in, and more fans than he could manage.

Can you imagine riding that high?

I suppose I had a spot of jealousy, thinking his life could never have been as hard as mine, that light and grace fell on his head at every moment. That's when Toby told the listeners, as if answering my thoughts, that life had not always been grand. That he had made mistakes, paid the price, and learned the lesson. Then he said, and this is what stuck with me, "You have to be where you are to get where you are going."

It set me back on my heels, as they say. Here was someone with everything—success, fame, fortune, family, and more fun than anyone should have—saying that life was not always perfect, but you can learn to live forward in the imperfection.

I decided at that moment to accept what I had created in my life and know, each time I wanted to yell, cry, or blame, that, while being where I was meant to be, I was getting where I was going.

There was freedom in that acceptance.

Many of my coaching clients come to me when things are upside down and when life is not what they want, but they can't quite find a way to get where they want to be. Many of the leaders I coach have staff who are not living up to expectations because life circumstances hobble them. I share Toby's simple sentence, *You have to be where you are to get where you are going,* and let it sink in for a moment. Then we talk about where they are and why. Then—and this is the part that excites me— we talk about where they are going and how the lessons they are learning now will serve them when they get there.

Life is a long and incredible journey, filled with highs and lows, tears and laughter. It is in the knowledge that tomorrow will be different from today that there is the greatest hope, an offering of faith that the best is yet to be.

I am older now and wiser. I have lived my whole life to get to this time and space, and guess what? It's not perfect, but oh, is it beautiful. Every lesson I have lived serves who I am now, makes me a better coach, wife, mother, friend, and human. I had to be there to get here, and I had to be here to get where I am going.

The same is true for you. You are right where you need to be to get where you need to go.

When you need to be honest with your people, when you need to say, "I see you, I know you, now get to work," they will hear you if they know you have their best interests at heart, which is how Quiet Leaders always work, not for themselves, but for the greater good, for the person or the community, they are serving.

I was lying in a lump on the physical therapy table. My legs
weren't working right, my back and hip hurt, and I was
whining, which is not really how I like to operate, but truth be
told I probably do it more than I should. When I say I abhor
helplessness, I mean in others, and my coaching clients will
attest to this. If they half-ass the work, or if they throw up their
hands and say, "I just can't," I drop them pretty quickly. If they
find the will, find the way, and if they do the work, I am all in!
But for me, well, truth be told, I kind of like to have help. I like
people to open the door for me (chivalry, please don't die!), and
I like when someone offers to show me a shortcut through the
terrain, especially if it's electronic terrain. If a hero wants to
ride in and save the day, I will cheer their arrival and lavish on
the thanks.

Yet helplessness is not my thing. I decided years ago to do the
work, forge the path, and do what I didn't think I could do. That
decision led me to today, the day I am sitting in my office
thinking about helping you to be a better leader, a Quiet Leader,
which takes me back to the physical therapy table.

At the time, we had a new puppy, one anxious to explore, chew,
and poo, so we put up a baby gate to keep her from the good
stuff. Well, in the bedrooms anyway. We are people who go,

not gather, so most of our property is not that great but still inappropriate for puppy explorations. Being a "goer," I was hurdling the gate each time I needed to go to the restroom or change my clothes, which can be 26 times a day. I would remind myself to go left, not right, with the hurdling leg, but not until the pain had crept in.

The hurdling soon took out my sacroiliac joint, causing incredible pain, which was not improved by the practitioner who yanked my leg so hard I almost fell off the table. Since that didn't work, I tried a fancy sort of massage, the type designed to move nerves around to improve their function. Right now, I am imagining my medical friends cringing that I went to a "witch doctor," and they should. The first massage was excellent, healing an old injury in my ribs. The second, well, that did move some things around, I guess. In the middle of the night, I woke with no feeling in my right foot. My primary caregiver, Cole Whitmoyer, DPN, who owns Flex Family Health, answered my 2:30 a.m. text message, calmed my adrenaline-fueled panic, and told me he'd see me in the morning.

I arrived at his office in tears. Not quiet tears either. Sobbing. Scaring my husband, whose only fear is me in warrior mode. Cole gave me a magnificent shot that eased the pain enough to start the healing and told me not to let anyone else touch me until this calmed down. He agreed I should see Josh Henderson, PT, DPT, ScD, OCS, for physical therapy when it did.

You better believe I was looking for help, hope, magic beans, anything and everything that would make me feel better when I got to Josh's. I could barely move; The pain had worn me out, and I was scared of what this could mean long-term. When Josh told me to bend, I bent, just not very far. When he told me to relax, I laughed and said that was impossible; I had too much to do, too much fear, and too much pain. He put his skills to work, moving, pressing, needling just the right spots. And he told me I had to work between sessions.

Work I did! Probably to the extreme for a while. Desperate to have the option to go where I wanted, when I wanted, without pain, as part of my life again, I stretched in the morning, in the evening, and did the strength-building exercises in the afternoon. I moved, soaked, massaged, and soon started to heal.

Then—and this is probably a character flaw I shouldn't reveal, but here we are—I kind of slacked off. During physical therapy visits, I felt the healing, the improvements, and so, really, did I need to do every exercise? I mean, all of them? Every day? It seemed a little much.

If you have been through physical therapy, you know that they know. The therapists see when you are trying, following their guidance, and they know when you are slacking. So there I was, whining. My leg was cattywampus to my torso, my eyes filling with tears as I felt a bit helpless and hopeless that this would never be over. That is when Josh, with all of the kindness and care I had come to appreciate him for, said, "Karen, you can't get stronger if you don't do things to make yourself stronger." Okay, so now honesty is part of the game too? Well then. What was I going to do with that little bit of wisdom?

I found myself thinking about it as I drove home and then as I did my exercises the next day.

Josh knew I could and should do more than I was doing, and he also knew that I was not a quitter. He had told me about patients who never did an exercise, hoping his ministrations could do it all. The patient often healed, but not in a timely manner. Sometimes they just lived with the injury and its results. We discussed the human proclivity to make excuses, take the easy out, and stop just before the end.

And, friend, isn't that leadership?

How often have you had high hopes for a person on your team, only to see them sit down just before they got to the finish line? How often have you had a dream for them, of healing, or winning, of finishing or smashing the competition, only to see them give in to doubt? It can be so hard to watch! But what Josh knew was that caring honesty is what I needed. I needed to know he knew I wasn't trying, and I needed to know he expected better results from me.

You can't get stronger if you don't do the things to make yourself stronger.

It is valid for your team, and it is true for you. There is work that needs to be done, truths that must be told, and finish lines that will only be crossed if you lean in and say, "Get your ass to work." Sure, sometimes a leader has to turn a blind eye and ignore the mess while embracing the possibilities. The work of a Quiet Leader is to do just that, sometimes. But more often than not, your job is to help your people do what they need to do for all the right reasons. Josh and Cole knew my goal was to be healthy and limber, and they knew it wasn't laziness or tomfoolery that would get me there. It was only time to heal and conscious, consistent, healthy effort that could help me feel like me again.

When you need to be honest with your people, when you need to say, "I see you, I know you, now get to work," they will hear you if they know you have their best interests at heart, which is how Quiet Leaders always work, not for themselves, but for the greater good, for the person or the community, they are serving. Honestly. Diligently. Serving.

Josh may never utter the words *You can't get stronger if you don't do the things to make yourself stronger* from a stage, or put them in a book—that's my job—but there is no doubt in my mind that when he uses them with a patient, it is the kindest, most powerful act of leadership I can imagine. It is true, it is simple, it is quiet, and it is right.

Now, go do the work to make yourself stronger. It is time for me to stretch and do the same.

Quiet Leadership

Change your seat. Change your perspective, and listen for the clarity it brings into your life.

SEATS

I often describe Helen as the little old lady who lived behind us when I was growing up. Recently, I had to come to grips with the fact that I am probably way older than she was during my childhood, but she *was* petite. And put together. And she was disciplined. And proper. And thrifty, oh, so thrifty! She made Kool-Aid with half the sugar called for, and baggies were saved, washed, and reused until they had holes worn in them. And she was always, always a lady. I fall short of her standards on many counts, yet I still find myself wanting to be like Helen.

You see, we had too many kids in too little space, too much chaos, and too much calling out of "seat back" when we got up for a drink of water during our Sunday night family Lawrence Welk and *Wonderful World of Disney* TV marathon. We called *seat back* because there were better spots than others, and a constant tumble to get those seats added to the chaos.

Helen's house was different. It was smaller than ours, cleaner than ours, and oh so much quieter than ours. You could only visit Helen when invited, and you had to be on your best behavior at all times or out the door you went. There were rules, and those rules were followed, by darn. I don't remember two of us kids ever being in her house simultaneously. When it was your turn to visit Helen, you entered through her neat-as-a-pin entry, and if you dropped sand on the way in, she swept it up before you were all the way down the short hall. You then got to sit on the wood box, as Helen cooked on a wood stove and got water from a pump in the kitchen sink.

While you were sitting there, Helen would sit across from you, on a small stool made with a tractor seat, and listen to your stories, asking great questions, offering feedback different than unreasonable parents, or she would busy herself with her chores. Monday was laundry day, and after drying the clothes on the line outside, she would sprinkle her husband Jack's shirts with water from a glass soda bottle and put them in the fridge overnight. On Tuesdays, she would iron the shirts with an iron heated on the woodstove. We didn't get to help, as these things need to be done correctly, but we did get to watch.

Both then and in retrospect, Helen's life seems perfect to me. It was calm, it was repetitive, filled with little moments of wonder, like finding that the flowers she planted in the rock wall had bloomed, or how hard you had to swing an ax to split the wood, something "little old" Helen did with ease, but I couldn't quite manage then or now. Her life gave me a new perspective on things, and it showed me there was another way to live, another way to manage life. There also was always another way to look at things when you were sitting in Helen's kitchen.

On special days, like when Dad was along, or it was your birthday, we would get to sit on the red folding stool. It was gleaming metal, with a vinyl seat and a fold-down step, and if I could find one today I would pay any amount for it, just for the memories. Everything was different when we sat on that seat, even in Helen's world where everything was the same from day to day, week to week, year to year. Sitting on that stool changed the perspective, made us the center of attention, offered us the chance to look at things from a new angle.

And that, above all the lessons I learned from Helen, was the Quiet Leadership lesson that has served me the best. That is the fact that changing your seat, changing the perspective from which you are looking at things, makes an incredible difference. I believe in this so much that I've written about it in each of my books. You see, we too often live like Helen, doing the same thing over and over, which is fine, unless you want different results. Helen didn't. Her life was her life, and it ran like clockwork. But when you are a leader and do or die is the state of affairs, the same ol' same ol' will not work. It is in sitting in a different seat, looking out a different window, asking a different question, that makes you a leader. It is in trying new things, being open to a complete 180, that creates growth. It is in doing things upside down and backward that helps us to right the ship, steady the compass, and find our way forward as leaders.

With her calm, simple life, Helen did that for me. She showed me the exact opposite of what I knew; she changed my seat and perspective and let me choose what was right for me. I do not live in a house as neat as a pin because the chaos I thought made me crazy actually gave me resilience, and I like the fact that there is a paint stain on my kitchen floor because that means I was creating when I could have been sitting with hands folded in my lap. I like that we know we should take our shoes off at the door, but we also know we can sweep up the debris later; we have things to do now. My house would make Helen uncomfortable, and that, I hope, would help her to look at things with a new perspective, just like her life did for me.

So, leader, while you are trying to figure out growth, while you are trying to figure out what the hell your team needs to move forward, or when you are scared, frustrated, or simply curious, sit in a new seat. Eat a different meal. Drive a different route. Ask a different question. Stand instead of sit, wonder instead of know. Listen instead of telling.

Change your seat. Change your perspective and listen for the clarity it brings into your life. Quietly.

Quiet Leadership

PART TWO   QUIETLY LEADING A TEAM

Ask more than you tell.

Act more than you direct.

Celebrate more than you correct.

There are three guidelines for leading as a Quiet Leader.

- **Ask more than you tell.**
- **Act more than you direct.**
- **Celebrate more than you correct.**

In our world, during this time of upheaval, unrest, and a dramatic readjusting, the best leaders, the ones putting up the results, are the ones that know where they are going and can politely move their team along with them. It is not a time for cajoling, pushing, or manipulating; this is a time for trusting, being flexible, and being positive.

We will discuss asking more than you tell in a following chapter, "Ask Three Questions." For now, I want you to know that when I discovered the system of asking three questions before I made a statement, a lesson I learned from my dad, I became a much more satisfied and much better leader, as well as a better human even.

I no longer shoved my passion or knowledge down people's throats simply because they were in my air space. I asked about them, what they hoped to learn, and how they hoped I could help them.

Often what they wanted to know or have me help them with was exactly what I wanted to impart to them. Still, in having the conversation and asking the questions, they became active listeners because they *asked* me to tell them. When I listened to them, I gave them only the information they needed, not all of the fluff and circumstance that went with my insights.

From that comes the idea of acting more than you direct. There was a time when leaders led, when standard training laid out the steps, the path, the rote learning ways to lead. *Set a vision, lay out the goals, call the plays, pass out only the necessary back pats.* Those ways were effective at the time, but now people want leaders they can work beside—leaders who walk the walk, dig the holes, pound the nails, and quiet the crying. In a world of TikTok videos and constant movement on every screen, at every hour, your people will glaze over and fall out of their chairs if you lecture them in an attempt to direct their actions. But (and this is what I hope you are doing), if you work beside them, or even behind them, letting them bask in all of the glory, you will become their favorite leader without even trying.

People are looking for action, forward movement from our leaders, authentic problem solving, and the active commitment to living the mission, day in and day out, from our leaders. Quietly leading is done without directing; it's done instead by inviting people to join you as you work with them.

As you contribute to the actual work, a Quiet Leader lavishes on the praise. Not only is this a kind practice, one that really can't be overdone, but it is also necessary in a world addicted to dopamine hits. From sugar in every food and beverage, to outrageous antics on our screens, to the constant action of a world that moves at 5G speed, people are addicted to dopamine. Kind and meaningful praise provides that dopamine fix.

I'm not suggesting celebration and praise be wasted, empty acts, but when you are busy looking for the best in your people, you can ignore the minor faults that matter only to you. When you celebrate the right actions, you will see more of them, and as a result, you will need to spend less time correcting the wrong actions. Now antagonistic banter and old-fashioned ribbing are only tolerated on social media. People are seldom looking for constructive feedback, which, to old-school leaders, seems counterintuitive to growth. Today's Quiet Leader knows that praise and celebration, used for the things that matter, can and will drive any mission forward and take any bottom line into the black. Growth happens when praise is sprinkled throughout the day; this is especially true if your team has members with trauma-damaged brains or high ACEs Scores (Harvard ACES Study: https://acestoohigh.com/got-your-ace-score/).

The last thing I want to come from Quiet Leadership is a set of rules, a mantra of proper leadership. We have tried that, and it no longer works. I want you to trust yourself and the knowledge you have gathered from the remarkable life you are living. I want you to listen to your grandpa and the homeless person on the street. Both have wisdom to give you, both know things about humans that you don't, things more significant than these three guidelines. Still, I think these guidelines will help you find your way and open the door to your journey as a Quiet Leader.

Ask more than you tell.
Act more than you direct.
Celebrate more than you correct.

You can lead quietly. And you will never regret it.

My advice is to love them anyway. But if you can—and this is really advice that is so much more effective—try not to hire them.

BLISTERS

I am going to put this out here, right in the beginning, because, friend, the sooner you know this, the sooner you accept this, the happier you will be as a leader.

Some people are like blisters; they only show up when all the work is done.

Now, isn't this a sad truth?

I am sure you have seen it play out time and again, both at work and play. Usually, there is one person on a team who pops in as you close the file and then stands there to claim the victory. They offer help when the project is finished, insert advice when it is not needed, and they conveniently *need* to leave to work with a client just before the real work gets assigned.

My advice is to love them anyway. But if you can—and this is really advice that is so much more effective—try not to hire them. I have never figured out the exact interview question to ferret out blisters. If you find it, let me know, but it is somewhere in there between *How do your team members describe your work style?* and *Are you a blister?*

In this book, you will discover many insights into the role of the Quiet Leader, and the one I will offer you now is never pop a blister, no matter how aggravating. You can cover it with a Band-Aid, or you can ignore it till it goes away, but popping a blister will ruin your reputation and land you in a heap of pain.

This advice is offered to you, Quiet Leader, with a wink and a grin.

"Now, Karen, people don't listen unless they asked to be told." Dad

My dad was a simple man. He had either a third-grade or an eighth-grade education, depending on the day he was telling the story, and he grew up with more sawdust than chalk on his hands. When he was 65 years old, he sent me a letter that said, *I am learning how to read and write*. I was completely blown away; as a child, I saw him read the newspaper every day, and each year he bought the latest set of encyclopedias because that was Google when I was a child. We could not get through our dinnertime conversations and arguments without looking something up.

Seeing my dad reading was just part of my life. But, in actuality, he was *pretending* to read so we would read and, as a result, have something he did NOT—a freedom to learn.

Fast-forward many years, and I was a well-paid business coach, traveling the country helping women become more successful. It may not surprise you to learn I was a bit full of myself. I knew it *all* about how to help them, and if people would just *listen* to me, they could have success.

Except people don't always listen, and even if they do, free will gives them the capacity to disappoint someone who *knows everything.* After a particularly harrowing coaching call, where clearly I was giving my best advice and it was falling on deaf ears, I hung up the phone, frustrated, sad for her that she could not grasp the wisdom I was pouring all over her.

I said—and this really was not one of my shining moments as a coach (the entire call had not been, truth be told)—"She is not, by damn, going to do a thing I told her."

My dad, sitting behind a book he was *actually* reading, said, "Now, Karen, people don't listen unless they asked to be told."

His statement kind of stopped me in my tracks. I loved to train consultative sales and used a lot of questions to help people get what they wanted in a purchase. I repeated my mantra: *You cannot convince people of anything; you can only give them information that helps them to make a decision, possibly the one you want, but you must accept their decision and stop trying to convince them,* often. Dad's words, that they didn't listen because they didn't ask for the lecture, dug to the root of my frustration and shone a light on *my* problem, not hers.

I had not asked what she wanted to learn or how she wanted to move forward, and I know this was a failure as a coach. Sure, I knew her goal, I knew she desired to move forward, but I did not know what was making the goal tick for her. I did not know precisely where she struggled or even why, besides the fact that I was such a *stellar* coach, she had turned to me for help.

My favorite book at the time was *The Question Behind the Question* by John G. Miller. His book was helping me to understand that if I was asked one question, there was generally another question, with more grit, right behind that one. So I thought to myself, what if I asked three questions before I started spouting wisdom? Would she have listened to me then?

So that is what I did. I called my client back, and was humbled that she even took my call. And I asked her three questions: *What was she struggling with? How was she hoping I could help? What did she need to move forward?* Then—and this is the part that makes me laugh—I told her the *exact* same things I had said on the earlier call, but I said them with more compassion and clarity in what she wanted to hear. I was also confident that what I said was really what she needed to hear; my demeanor had changed for the better—because I asked questions.

That afternoon changed everything about my coaching and training. I asked more and better questions, I used fewer words to help people move forward, and together we saw better results. I simply asked a few questions to get the person's buy-in. They immediately knew I had their best interests at heart because I had listened to them before I poured my verbose brilliance all over them.

Since then, I have trained thousands of people to ask three questions before they make a statement. Similarly, I suggest that they ask more questions of their children, spouse, and staff, not just their clients. It takes a bit of practice to get comfortable asking more questions, so here are three ideas to make this work:

Practice with everyone you see. On the bus, in a restaurant, in your classroom, ask them three questions when the stakes are *not* high, and you will become more confident of your skills when they *are* high.

Do not ask accusatory questions. I like to tease that for some reason when we say *Why did you do that,* or *What the heck were you thinking?* the results diminish; this is especially true with spouses, I have found. Instead, ask *Can you tell me what happened, tell me how you are thinking of handling this, how can I help, how are you dealing with this, what do you want me to know?* There are a thousand questions to help people grow; just ask them carefully, with *their* best interest at heart. That is the magic of communication.

Let them answer. Do NOT (and this is especially hard if, like me, you kind of know *everything,* and you are *sure* you understand the answer they need before they have even formulated the question) answer before they finish speaking. *Shhhh.* You asked the question, so be quiet and let them talk. It will be your turn soon enough.

I will tell you that becoming a better question-asker has not been without its pains. Sometimes people will tell you EVERYthing. EVERY damn thing. So do not ask a question to which you do not want to know the answer. In the same vein, do not ask a question that points out how much more you know than them; trickery does not build trust. My husband also likes to remind me not to ask questions in places where they just might think I am too nosey for my own good, like back alleys and cafes in the middle of nowhere.

Kidding aside, do know that when you are working with someone, as a coach, mentor, or friend, it might take more than three questions; it might take ten. Still, once you learn to ask better questions *before launching*, you will find that the magic happens, and the person you are talking to will say, "What do you think?" or "What do you know about this subject?" That, my friend, is the magical moment when you *get* to launch because *they* ASKED you to tell them. *They* want to know what you know, what you are thinking, or what can teach them.

Use your power well.

Do not tell them irrelevant things or things not in their best interest. You will eradicate all of the goodwill your questions gained you if you do. If you give solid answers that feed into *their* needs, they will listen because they asked to be told in that glorious moment of communication, just like my dad, the man who reads people better than books, said they would.

For more by Karen Grosz, go to canvascreekteams.com, QuietLeadership.group, or Amazon, where you will find **What's Next?** *and* **Seasoned.**

...ask yourself if your people know that when you ask them how they are, that you care, as if their life depended on it.

AS IF THEIR LIFE DEPENDED ON IT

The idea of being underwater, of breathing through a manmade contraption, having to know my depth, the pounds of air in my tank, the hand signal for when I spy a lionfish, as well as the one for I'm out of air, which apparently is not to be given in a thrashing fit, overwhelms me. The oceanic world may be cool, but really, could it be that cool?

My family says yes to diving. Hundreds of people at the resort where I am writing this chapter and millions worldwide also say yes. Still, it just does not interest me. I am more than happy sitting on the boat waiting for my people to surface or standing on the beach watching the sunrise as they leave for their adventure and then listening to them exclaim, upon their return, of the sights they saw, the difficulties they overcame. But going with them, nope, not interested.

As I sit and observe the getting ready, then the dive review, what interests me is the Quiet Leadership their dive masters display. Each dive master I have observed has one main characteristic: confidence. They know precisely where their gear is. They trust the captain to know where they will dive and that they'll be in the right location when they surface. They know all of the details, all of the signals, and all of the best spots to spy on the most elusive creatures. The dive masters I've observed, with one exception, are not braggadocios or full of false bravado. The braggadocious one seemed to have wavering support of his followers. Dive masters have a confident style of leadership that experience has given them.

The dive masters ask each person, as if their life depended on it, how they are doing. It's not a cursory "how are ya," but a true, give-me-the-facts question, to which they intently listen to the answer. That answer can be the difference between life and death. They assess how much weight the diver will need based on their size and the conditions, and after readying all the details, they brief their team of divers on where they will go, what they will see, and how they are to behave while underwater. Some things they'll see can be touched; some cannot. Sometimes you can stray from the group; sometimes you must stay in a tight group, acting as a school of fish as they dart around the underwater gardens. There is no *if you want to*, or *I suggest*; instead, there is a calm authority that you will, without an argument, do as I am instructing you if you want to come back alive.

Diving is a dangerous activity that is full of fun and laughter if you listen to the dive master.

I have never feared for the lives of my divers, except when Mr. Braggadocious was in charge. The dive masters know their craft, understand their responsibilities, and expect their team to do as they instructed them. And their team of divers has utter respect for them. They listen, ask questions, and at the end of the dive, if something did not go quite right, they take the feedback the master gives them and adjust their style, gear, or behavior to meet the expectations. They do this because they know doing so means the master will bring them back alive, with stories to tell.

Oh, such leadership.

Once underwater, every direction or correction is given silently with nods, points, hand signals, or a firm tap on the arm from time to time. The master has no room for doubt, no tolerance for hijinks, and has the ultimate authority to end a dive at a moment's notice. And time and again, the master will point out the beautiful corals, the lively and the shy fish, and warn divers with the signal for lionfish (which I still don't know because I don't dive). Dive masters want you not just to breathe but to live and to expand your love of the oceans and the life they contain.

Oh, such leadership.

It is like waves on an ocean, steady, consistent, powerful.

Breathe in.

Breathe out.

Relax.

Follow me.

Breathe in. Breathe out. Relax. Follow me. Breathe in. Breathe out. Relax. Follow me. Breathe in. Breathe Out. Relax. Follow me.

You, too, Quiet Leader, probably embody many of these things. Your team knows your facial expressions, your mannerisms, and what they do that makes you, their leader, want to *call the dive off* and end their time on your team. But do they know, without a doubt, that you are there to keep them safe? Do they know that you are leading them because you know where they are going, what they need in order to get there, and that you will keep them safe along the way? Do they have enough trust in you to put a regulator in their mouth, breathe air from a tank you filled, and follow you through a cavern called the Devil's Throat?

Dive masters establish their leadership with a team in minutes, first, because of their title. All divers know the hours that went into achieving that rank, what they studied, what they accomplished as part of their title. That title deserves and earns respect from their divers. Second, because of their manner: quiet, efficient, factual, steady, informative. A good dose of humor is a welcome bonus.

The only master I have seen lose their unquestioned authority was more concerned about their own dive experience, about their own reputation; they wanted to be honored by the group instead of earning their respect. While that attitude has been rare on a boat, in my experience it seems to be rampant here above the water, in boardrooms and offices everywhere. Leaders often demand to be honored instead of stepping back and earning their followers' respect.

If you are trying to be a better leader, one with quiet and humble authority, one who can, in minutes, establish that your leadership is pure and followable, you may want to take up scuba diving. Give yourself over to watching another leader, in a completely different setting, one who is keeping you alive, leading you through what could be a story to tell or an unthinkable disaster, and learn from their example. While you are watching them and trusting your life to their guiding ability, ask yourself if your people know that when you ask them how they are, that you care, as if their life depended on it.

That's what a dive master does. That's what a Quiet Leader does.

So, my first lesson in Quiet Leadership was knowing when to keep your mouth shut, when to look the other way, and why you always want to ask yourself if the fight is worth the battle.

TUNA CANS

Way back before I thought of being an author, back when I was first learning to be me, I wanted to do the hardest thing I could think of, to help me grow professionally, and truth be told to make a lot of money. This was back in the day of want ads and cell phones the size of candy bars, which I had, a red cell phone that was the size of a Snickers bar. There were no cameras, no texting, and no social media. I mean way back, after color TV, but before Facebook. That's when I learned my first, original lesson in Quiet Leadership—Tuna Cans, the one that started it all.

When you are in the car business, you work a lot of hours because you never want to miss an "Up" or a "Be Back" because, frankly, making a lot of money requires a lot of both Ups and Be Backs, and you are seldom sure when they will arrive. An Up is a first-time shopper, and the next salesperson in line gets to *get up* and help them. A Be Back is a return customer, one who said, "I'll be back," which, once you've been in sales for more than a month, you realize is usually a lie. When a Be Back *actually* comes back, well Nelly, hold the horses; a sale is about to happen!

Now that you know these fascinating facts, it's time to tell you another. Lunch is essential to car salespeople, at least it was at the dealership where I worked. We started talking about lunch when we first walked in the door; we would talk about it when customers thought we were having the all-important "talk with my manager," and we would talk about it two hours after we ate it. Where to order, what to order, what we had last time, when to order, who would buy, and who would pick up were conversations important enough to keep us going when Ups and Be Backs were few and far between.

No one worked longer hours or better understood where and what to order for lunch than our general manager, Dave. Dave had been born for the car business and had been in it longer than any of us. He knew people, how to sell to them, how to treat them, how to make an extra grand or two off them, and more importantly, how to feed them so they stuck around to make the next sale. Dave entered the dealership on his first day with a file full of menus, a phone full of restaurant phone numbers, and a reputation for taking care of the customer like few others ever could. We loved him beyond measure for all these things: the lessons, the connections, the meals, the humor, and his never-quit attitude.

Still, from time to time, no matter how badly we wanted to be there for the next Be Back, our families needed our attention, and Dave's family was no different. His beautiful wife, Patty, drove a white Suburban with pipes that shook the high-class neighborhood they lived in, and she skillfully shuttled their four children through active school and sports lives while Dave moved rolling metal. When Dave's cheerful attitude slipped a few notches, he decided to take a long weekend, which is almost unheard of in the industry. Sure, the owner could take a long weekend, so could the mechanics, but the sales team was supposed to be on high alert, making sales when Ups and Be Backs graced our lot, which usually started on Fridays around 3:00 p.m.

After a busy weekend, we looked forward to Dave's return on Tuesday, confident he'd be so happy that he'd buy lunch and tell us a story or two while we ate too many calories.

We were wrong. Dave, a big man anyway, came in like a bear, growling, snapping, and swiping at us when we asked about lunch. Finally, I said, "What the hell, man? You are in worse shape now than when you left last week." Dave reported that on Friday, day one of vacation, Patty made tuna sandwiches for lunch, and she didn't rinse the cans before she put them in the trash compactor. Now, trash compactors were a big deal then, but they seem to have lost their luster now, primarily because of their propensity to get stinky before you had to take out the bag of compressed and decomposing deposits.

Tuna cans—well, they have a stench all their own before you even slide them into the receptacle, so Dave told Patty that she needed to rinse the cans before she put them in the compactor. Patty suggested she did not; she had a lot of things to do to feed their hungry family, and this step was a waste of time. Furthermore, if he was so concerned about the tuna cans, he could rinse them out himself.

You know how these things go; you say one thing, they say another, and pretty soon no one is speaking, and someone is sleeping on the couch.

So, Dave spent time sleeping on the couch. I, being much more hesitant to start a fight, let alone stay in one, was both shocked and impressed. Staying mad, or continuing to be an ass for that long, took stamina I don't have in my marriage. We are over most things in 3.2 seconds. When I asked Dave if I could use this story, he didn't remember it, which is the blessing of a good love story; you forget the days that stunk and remember those that didn't.

Anyway, Dave said, "I now realize that I let a little thing, a tuna can, something I could have rinsed out, or better yet never mentioned, ruin an excellent thing."

From that moment on in the dealership, "Tuna Can" became code for "Its just a little thing," inconsequential in the overall goal of moving metal, building relationships. As soon as someone would start to grumble, we'd ask them, "Is this just a Tuna Can?" and most of the time they would back down, look at what truly mattered, and move forward with a cheerful demeanor, similar to Dave's.

So, my first lesson in Quiet Leadership was knowing when to keep your mouth shut, when to look the other way, and why you always want to ask yourself if the fight is worth the battle. Sometimes, as leaders, we have to speak up. We have to stand our ground, step into the fray, or lay down the law. But, usually, we don't have to stick there. We don't have to draw the line so firmly that sleeping on the couch or ousting the employee is our only recourse. We can step back, ask what matters, and, in many cases, offer to help with the Tuna Cans instead of creating a problem where one doesn't need to exist.

Don't let the little things ruin the big things. Tuna Cans is a lesson that doesn't stink.

…sometimes fixed is not the fairy tale ending you hope it will be. Sometimes we can address the problems, adjust the processes, smooth the waters, but in the end, what you hoped fixed would look like is not what you get. I don't think that is a failure; it is a different solution.

FIX IT

Sometimes everything feels broken. Communication has stopped, team members are leaving, sales are down, and the dream no longer sparkles. Usually, this is when leaders call me to help them and their teams to move forward, sort of a last-ditch effort to right the ship. I wish they would have called earlier, of course, but still, I jump on my trusty paintbrush and ride to their side, hoping I can save the day. Often I do. And sometimes I don't.

Did I fail? Sometimes. Did they quit? Sometimes. Was it hopeless? Sometimes. Do we score points for trying? Yes! Did we fix it? Always. Let me explain.

When someone says, "I want to fix this," the biggest thing I want to know is what "this" is. Is it the bottom line, the culture, the systems, the relationships; what exactly will be "fixed?" Sometimes that is hard to determine. When things feel broken, they simply and exhaustedly feel broken. The drum has lost its beat, the color has lost its hue, and usually, everyone has a different example of the brokenness, so we start the investigation. When did it feel whole? What did healthy look like? What would "fixed" look like? Once we design the outcome, we work on the plan and its execution.

So, Quiet Leader, this is what I want you to know. If you feel like you want to "fix this" because it's just not right anymore, first you have to ask yourself what is wrong. Then you have to ask yourself what "fixed" looks like, what you are working to achieve. But here is the thing that is always hardest to hear: sometimes fixed is not the fairy tale ending you hope it will be. Sometimes we can address the problems, adjust the processes, smooth the waters, but in the end, what you hoped fixed would look like is not what you get. I don't think that is a failure; it is a different solution.

Sometimes fixed is leaving. Sometimes it is in saying good-bye to people, tired systems, the team, or the business.

Sometimes fixed involves a break, which is okay because that too is a type of fix. As you move forward, you and your team should prepare for *fixed* to be utterly different from what you had, yet incredibly beautiful for its newness. I respect your need for fixed but want to remind you that the most potent cycle in the world is order, disorder, reorder. The cycle does not take you back to what you had; it takes you through a process of questioning, adjusting, trying, failing, and succeeding until finally, you enter reorder, the most beautiful stage.

It is in the moments when disorder feels the most chaotic and painful that you and your team will naturally cry out, "Fix this." Then, while settling into reorder, you will realize that what broke needed to break and that fixed becomes the new state of order, eventually giving way to disorder. Again, this is the natural, although sometimes tumultuous march of time and growth, and it does not need to be fixed because it is not broken.

When a team asks me to help them *fix it,* when they stand shoulder to shoulder and declare that is what they want to do, that is when I get excited, when I know change is about to happen. It takes commitment and grit to "fix it." Fixing it starts in the hearts of the leader and their team. Fixing it cannot be done without trust, and trust won't be gained without honesty. If one team member is wishy-washy on the desire to "fix it," the outcome is less than stellar. That is where grit comes in, in the hard conversations about who is in and who is out, and letting the truths fall where they may. It takes love, grace, and commitment to the idea of being whole. When a team has that, then "fixed," no matter how similar or how different it is than before, it is not just attainable; it is inevitable.

You need to employ four things when you undertake a "fix it" project.

Raw honesty about what broke. I don't care how it broke or who was responsible; all we need is honesty about the solution and the process of finding it.

Commitment. There is no time for wavering unless you want the fix to remain an unattainable dream. Every person on the Fix-It Squad has to be 100% in, 100% committed to disorder, and reorder.

The ability to collaborate. The fix is like collaborative art; in the beginning, no one understands what they can offer or how the task will be completed. As the work unfolds, they realize they have to yield to splashes of brilliance, and they have to admit that they alone don't hold the answers, that it is in giving and taking, adding and changing so that the right art, the right solution creates itself.

Absolute pragmatism. Everything is going to be okay. Everything and everyone. It might be different, but in the end, it is what it is. Pragmatism does not mean a lack of caring or a lack of pride; instead, it allows space for error, listening, growth, and probably most importantly, for laughing as yet another quick fix crashes and the next one bubbles to the surface.

I know you want it fixed, and so does your team, and it will be; it just might be different than it was before it broke, and you will stand side by side and revel in that fact.

Getting what you expect is equal parts setting and clarifying appropriate expectations and looking for the best, not the worst, in every situation.

When was the last time you yelled at the person driving in front of you? For most people, it was the last time they were in the car. That other driver was too slow, too erratic, too in the way, and someone needed to hear about it. Them. When was the last time you had lousy service in a restaurant? Found a hair on your hotel shower curtain? Felt let down by the person who was supposed to be providing stellar service? When was the conference room too cold, too hot, or too dark? When did you need to complain about something, anything, or everything?

If it is always, constantly, or even three times today, I would say—and I hope you will take this in the loving tone I mean to offer it with—you are getting exactly what you expect.

If you expect to see bad drivers, you will see bad drivers. If you expect lousy service, cold food, warm beer, and one person after another who cannot seem to do their job right, it is because that is what you are looking for, my friend.

You get what you expect.

If you expect the world to shit on you, it will.

If you expect humans to let you down, they will, one right after the other.

You will find that the world rises to meet your expectations.

I often talk about registering for a conference; you know there will be a plated meal. Often, especially in beef country, people whine "They're probably going to serve chicken," with a defeated tone. When the chicken arrives, no matter how beautifully plated, it is easy for them to lean to the person on the right and say, "Chicken, I just knew it," with the satisfaction of a disgusted tone.

I like to suggest another approach with the same scenario but wildly different results. When registering, if you think to yourself, "Gosh, I wonder if they will serve chicken?" with an optimistic outlook, you will feel like screaming, in excited tones, "CHICKEN!" when it arrives. Leaning to the person on the right elicits an "I knew it! I just knew it! Chicken, can you even believe it?!" with the excited tone of picking the right choice.

Both settings are exactly the same, chicken for dinner, but one is better for your blood pressure, mood, and reputation. Few people choose a grump as their leader, and if the grump is their leader, they decide to have as little interaction as possible with that leader.

Now, I am often accused of being Pollyanna, but I'm more in tune with the term *happily pragmatic*. Yes, there will be people who drive poorly, and there will be people who can't get an order straight, and there will be people who let you down, no matter how optimistic your expectations.

Still, looking for the light in the world, the best in humans, the positive in a flood of negatives, makes life easier, more joy-filled.

When I get in the car, I expect people to drive the best they can in their situation. Maybe they are new in town; perhaps they are racing to an injured child; maybe they are being directed by a drunken Siri who is slow and slurring. When I expect that people are doing the best they can, I don't have to yell at them; I can instead allow them to cut in front of me, turn erratically, perhaps causing chaos, and go on about my day with nary a complaint.

Similarly, in a restaurant, I have no idea how many special requests the waitstaff is dealing with, if they just suffered a nasty breakup, or if Aunt Peg is at a table around the corner.

You see, Aunt Peg (name changed to protect familial harmony, plus she scares me just a bit) could drive anyone to drink and any waitstaff to regret their career choice. Aunt Peg never received a drink that was made correctly; no steak was ever eaten without returning it to the grill first. Receipts were not scanned; they were audited. At an upscale restaurant in Hawaii, I once watched her return three drinks. The third time, the waitress stood at the bar, holding the drink, before returning to the table with a drink with no changes. The waitress gave Aunt Peg a commiserating, long-suffering eye roll, apologized for the new bartender, and Aunt Peg, satisfied with the attention, and the acknowledgment of the incompetence that she had to suffer through, approved the drink with raves.

Now, if that waitress is also dealing with a gluten-free by choice, a side of ranch, two over-drinkers, and a picky child at every table, as well as Aunt Peg, things are going to break down somewhere.

Instead of carping about the situation, be happily pragmatic. Appreciate that you are in a position where you can be served instead of serving, that you won't be washing dishes, and that there is a wondrous amount of background work that actually got your food to your plate—from seed to box, box to distributor, and menu creator, delivery driver, chef, and waitstaff. They are just a few of the people providing your gastric pleasures. Imagine that! It is worth ignoring, with a smile and a wave of the hand, if something is not quite perfect.

As a leader, you have expectations of your team. Ways they behave, show up in the world, and should serve your mission. It helps if you are completely clear with them what those expectations are. No one can hit a target they can't see. If you expect timeliness, be timely. If you expect them to live the mission, make sure it is on the wall where they can see it and part of every decision. Tell them if you expect dedication, growth, input, or blind march step behavior. People will strive to meet reasonable expectations that you have clearly communicated.

That clear communication means that you, the Quiet Leader, will get what you expect, and that is a wonderful feeling. Getting what you expect is equal parts setting and clarifying appropriate expectations and looking for the best, not the worst, in every situation.

I would be remiss if I didn't share this tidbit with you. I have high expectations of the people in my world. I expect them to meet my standards, do it with a smile, and never let me down. It's not always reasonable, because people are people, which is why I try to lead with happy pragmatism. Still, I found that I was a bit let down, a bit disappointed in several things, and it put me in a bit of a funk.

Listening to a podcast, I heard the host say they decided to lead with appreciation over expectations. It was one of those crystallizing moments of clarity, and I knew I needed to change my expectation of myself and those around me in that instant.

So I practiced leading with appreciation before expectation. Appreciation of the driver doing a good job, the staff person creating a win, the family member lending a hand. I appreciated all of those things, above expecting those things.

It has been a wondrous transformation. I still expect the best, look for the brightest, find the silver lining, but in appreciating those things before expecting them, they have shown up faster, brighter, and with more dramatic results.

So you get what you expect, yes, but if you appreciate what you expect, well, that truly can change your attitude towards life!

She doesn't say a word, although sometimes there is an excited yip; there is just silent communication of her expectations, your role in filling them, and her joy when you follow her lead.

DROP THE BALL

There are dogs that rescue people, dogs that sniff out drugs, dogs that just travel around in purses, dogs that herd cattle, and dogs that seem to do nothing at all.

Then there are dogs that play ball.

We have one of those dogs. A Labrador pup named Katmai, half black, half chocolate, a mix we lovingly call dark chocolate. Katmai was named for a river in Alaska, a place with bears, fish, and stories best told with a glass of whiskey, which seems fitting because Katmai can drive a teetotaler to drink with her insistent need to chase a ball.

I know, I know, we introduced her to it, and we even encouraged it. Together, Paul and I bear the brunt of knowing full well that her addiction to chasing a ball is all our fault because we threw the first one, and we pay the price *every single day* for that action.

150

But when you sit back and watch, when you see her joy as she bounds after the ball, if you watch as she drops it time and again in front of her victim, I mean playmate, you see a damn fine example of Quiet Leadership.

She doesn't say a word, although sometimes there is an excited yip; there is just silent communication of her expectations, your role in filling them, and her joy when you follow her lead.

She has a vision, to chase the ball, and you have a role, to throw the ball, and then, because often this is what leadership involves, she brings the ball right back to you, with a wiggle of her butt and expectant eyes, so that you can throw it again.

Leaders do that. Quite ones anyway. They don't change the game, and they don't muddy the waters by changing direction when staying on task will do the trick. They drop the ball and let their people know that throwing it, again and again and again and again, is precisely what they want them to do.

Quiet Leaders know that sometimes they are wrong, sometimes they are right, but they are always at their best if they are focused on giving everyone involved a piece of the win.

ROCKS AND HARD PLACES

Do you know how many lawyer jokes there are? Three—all the others are true. That is one of my favorite jokes, partly because I can remember it, and partly because it is so universal. You can switch lawyer for blonde, plumber's crack, or any other grouping, and it always gets a laugh. While I love to joke about them, I have to tell you, I do admire a good lawyer, a profession that includes many of my friends and clients. Lawyers stand up for what's right as well as for what might not be quite right, but they are contractually obligated to defend and they will go toe to toe and chest-deep into conflict.

Not me.

I know, I am a Karen, and we are supposed to be the reigning queens of conflict, especially if there is a manager around. I do believe that right is right and wrong is wrong, and that somebody should do something about injustice, bullies, and those who are overcharging for services rendered. I am just not going to start the fight, and I am probably going to let my

154

adversary win just to keep the peace, if it's not that big a deal. It's how I say happily pragmatic.

However, the last time I remember raising my voice in anger was pretty epic, and well deserved. My dear husband, Paul, had been out of the hospital for less than two hours, following the 14-foot crash to the floor that we call the Fall with Jesus, when he climbed a flight of stairs with a friend's help after I'd expressly said we'd follow the doctor's orders of no stair climbing. Telling Paul and his friend, in no uncertain terms, exactly how I felt about the situation, which included imploring the friend to (insert blue language) shut up and take a seat, a directive he quickly followed, was not a stellar day in my book. There are better ways to deal with conflict, even though Paul thought I was "sexy as hell in warrior mode."

It's funny, then, that I spend a fair amount of my consulting time helping people to deal with conflict. If there is a rock and hard place, I am going to go around it. If we are stuck in the mud and the mire, I am going to walk to town to find help. If the problem is miscommunication, I am probably going to point out that I communicate for a living, and so it is probably the other person's problem, which elicits a big guffaw every time. I have a hundred reasons to avoid negative conflict, but the biggest one is this: I think it's avoidable.

One of the reasons I am drawn to be a Rotarian is the Four-Way Test. This asks, of the things we think say or do:

- Is it the truth
- Is it fair to all concerned?
- Will it build goodwill and better friendships?
- Will it be beneficial to all concerned?

For me, if the statement, the action, the policy, does not pass the Four-Way test, why would you do it? Passing the test avoids negative conflict. Similarly, the Ten Commandments lay out some pretty good ground rules for getting along as humans.

But we don't always follow those guides, and sometimes, even with the best intentions, we end up conflicted, fighting, and in a mess of words, some of which shouldn't be uttered and others that can't seem to be spoken. Not only do I think it is best to avoid conflict, but I think most of the time we *can* avoid it.

I should point out that I am a huge fan of constructive conflict.

Big discussions, push and pull conversations where both sides are heard, theories are challenged, and concepts are batted around—those I love. That sort of healthy conflict is productive, constructive, and necessary for positive and powerful growth. The conflict that ends in hurt feelings, slammed doors, resignations, and silent treatments is destructive, and what I want to discuss with you now.

First, as a Quiet Leader, I would argue that you can avoid most negative conflict situations with clear communication, processes that eliminate margins for error, and—this may or may not surprise you—the willingness to be pragmatic and let things roll off your back. Not every situation is right or wrong, my way or the highway. Few things (except maybe rocket science and brain surgery) need to be dealt with in a "the" way, not "a" way type of attitude. Communication breakdowns are more often than not caused because the listener, the intended recipient of the communication, either did not feel the need or did not feel comfortable enough to ask clarifying questions.

When your organization has a culture of excellence, excellence can only be delivered if policy, procedure, and communication are designed to support that excellence, and if there is support for uninterrupted questioning of unclear communication.

Second, when a Quiet Leader finds themselves in a conflict situation, there are three things that are going to get them out of it. The first is a fast car. (Kidding. Don't cut and run; that is seldom the correct solution.) The real tools you most often need to solve a conflict are honesty, vulnerability and empathy.

It takes a big person to admit when they made a mistake, or simply don't understand the problem. The vulnerability comes in when you talk about how the conflict affects you, and why you want to solve it. Empathy is the most important, but the easiest to overlook. When you, as the leader, take time to understand the pain, to feel for the other(s), and to own your part of the solution, conflict winds down quickly.

Once those three things are in place, I believe teams need time to talk.

First, they need to talk about who they are as individuals, what they like, don't like, what they do for fun. I ask people to tell the group a story that makes them who they are today.

Second, the team needs to know that from this point forward, from the time of the initial meeting about the conflict, all conversations are geared towards moving forward. Sure, you can discuss the reason you got into this pickle, but that has probably been done so often you can recite one another's lines and they have become Dead Cats. Dead Cats are the things we carry around that everyone is sick of looking at, hearing about, and dealing with. (For more on Dead Cats, see my book *What's Next*. Reading that chapter to warring teams has calmed many a tumultuous storm.)

Third, rapid change is important. Teams in crisis want to fix something and promising to fix it "someday" just fans the flames. Pick three easy wins, three targets that can be bull's-eyed immediately, and put them into play. I recently worked with a team of lawyers, and the chief complaint, the easiest target, was communication. They were all so focused on work that they didn't stop to look one another in the eye, and they weren't taking time to share either their struggles or their wins. We instituted morning huddles the next day, and we saw results the next day. Within a matter of hours, those 15-minute meetings solved a myriad of problems and added not just communication back to their workday, but laughter.

Resolving conflict is seldom accomplished overnight, but the work is worth the effort. Teams who face negative conflict head on are stronger in the end, and more apt to welcome constructive conflict as part of their normal pattern. Giving each person space to be heard, looking for solutions instead of causes, and a pragmatic but determined attitude to be part of the solution are the first and most important steps. Quiet Leaders usually do these things naturally, because Quiet Leaders know that sometimes they are wrong, sometimes they are right, but they are always at their best if they are focused on giving everyone involved a piece of the win. Staying out of the lawyer's office isn't a bad goal either.

People will do what you celebrate.
Celebrate carefully and often.

One of the things that has given me success as a trainer and a coach is the ability to break things down to their most basic level. I feel that when someone listens to you, works with you, wants to move forward using the advice you have given them, that there is nothing more powerful than when they say, "I can do that!" I've developed entire training events around the concept; I can do that! Think about the last time you heard one of your people use that sentence. There is no defeat in their voice, no whiney "I don't know how I'll get this done." There is just unmitigated freedom in the knowledge that they can and will move forward because you helped them to see the most basic steps necessary.

To inspire that "I can do that" moment, define what you see as stumbling blocks, and then determine how you can use them to your advantage. What is the silver lining of tripping over them? Then determine what the first, smallest action item is. Once that is accomplished you move on to the next best step, never worrying about all of the steps, only the next one.

"I can do that" takes the smallest action and turns it into results, one small step at a time. Sometimes those steps crumble, so you have to begin again. Read on for more about that idea.

I think there is beauty in simplicity, which is why I want to share these two ideas with you. The first is one I'd heard before but never really thought about until recently, when I was working with my health coach: the kind and empowering words "Begin again."

Begin again. You don't need to beat up yourself (or your people) over a mistake or a failed attempt; you can simply begin again. Use the knowledge you gained through failure to bring about different results. Use the first attempt to make the second attempt go more quickly or smoothly. Don't overthink, and don't pull it apart, terrorizing yourself with "what if" and "I should have." Stop the cycle by starting again.

When I wrote my first book, I had heard it takes 87 drafts before you have something worth sharing. I thought to myself, that might be true for others, but I am a speedy, get-it-down-and-done kind of writer, and I would not need 87 drafts. On my 85th draft, I relented and admitted that I needed to begin again. And when I did, the result was much clearer, much more straightforward, and inspired people to say, "I can do that," which is precisely what I wanted to have happen. Begin again. It's not going to be as painful as you think, and you can do that too.

As long as we are talking about simplicity, and using it to move you and your team forward, think about this: it's as simple as it can get.

People will do what you celebrate. I know, that's pretty basic. But actually, it's not basic when you put it solidly into practice. If you are unhappy with a team member who is constantly in your office, telling you the woes of living the life they live or working with the people they work with, it is because you celebrate them with your attention. That is why they are there and why they are telling you the story, again. They feel celebrated when you commiserate, wipe their tears, or hold their hand.

You also see these results on the sales floor, in recruiting efforts, and in any other situation where achievement requires action, not procrastination. If people are not hitting the mark, and you talk about it, train about it, carp, and wring your hands about it, that is, in a weird way, celebration.

What works better is to break down the result you want into its most basic "I can do that" steps, figure out which step is the most effective, then cheer, celebrate, and hold up as an example when that positive step is accomplished. Those are the conversations to host in your office, not the "My coworkers are useless, and I am not the problem" drivel that can take too much of your time.

If it takes 20 calls to land a client, celebrate the dials. If it takes 20 Tweets to get attention, celebrate the twittering. When you see the right action, praise it! Note whenever your team is doing something you want to see repeated.

If I hold regular meetings with a team, especially one with a penchant for tardiness, I always have a small gift for the first three people to arrive in the room. I don't talk about it ahead of time; the people who arrived first will do that for me when they show it off. The next time we meet, more people will arrive before the appointed hour, hoping for their little celebration. If we need to have a conversation and the team is hard-pressed to speak up, tossing chocolate to the first few who share gets the wheels greased and the conversation flowing. Now, you might think a board president is going to roll their eyes at a tactic like that, but I'm telling you, they didn't become president without a bit of competition in their veins, and if chocolate is on the line and all they have to do is speak, well they will have chocolate.

The thing is, celebration does not have to be big or fancy; I really want you thinking "I can do that" about celebrating what you want to see repeated. If you want your people to be on time, don't yelp when they are late; cheer when they are early. If you want them to follow up, don't ask why it didn't happen; reward them for dialing the phone. If you want them to recruit, cheer identifying potentials; if you want them to exercise, challenge them to a crunch-off, don't criticize them for needing a larger size uniform. Celebrate what you want to see repeated, again and again, and again, until the behavior becomes the norm.

Quiet Leadership takes on many forms, as many forms as there are leaders, but I think this type of Quiet Leadership, the base actions of simplicity, is one of the best. Knowing the very base of what will get results, celebrating that, and doing it again and again, quietly, and sometimes loudly; however you feel like expressing your joy that your leadership is working, do that.

Again and again. People will do what you celebrate. Celebrate carefully and often.

When you embrace "I can do that" moments, the idea of beginning again, and celebrating what you want to see repeated, you and your team will stand proud, and accomplished because of the work you do together.

Quiet Leadership

There is a day when you decide that you, the person doing the work, is just as important as the work. That you, the person with so much to give, is worthy of a recipient who cares about you as much as you do about them.

KITCHEN DUTY

I drove into Luccock Park with my daughter, Liz, and two-year-old grandson, Ezra, expecting to see a classic church camp, maybe a few old buildings, big trees, and space to play. What I didn't expect was an incredible view from east to west, a seven-acre meadow, and a feeling of complete calm and confidence, something I am always seeking.

I had been invited to Luccock for an hour to help with the agenda for RYLA (Rotary Youth Leadership Award) and to discuss doing a bit of team building for them later in the summer. Little did I know this would soon become the work of my heart. Today, twelve years later, I am sitting on the porch of the manager's cabin at Luccock while our pup chews on a bone, and my husband catches a few more hours of rest in a place that is silent except for bird calls and the rolling gurgle of the small creek.

I like hard work, but I have never worked harder in my life than I do here at Luccock. I like a challenge, and boy howdy have those been offered in spades. Most of all, I love to grow people, and the possibilities to facilitate that have been incredible in this sacred space. Part of developing people is watching and listening as life's quiet lessons unfold around me, which happened in the kitchen here.

I had never been tasked with overseeing a commercial kitchen before; in fact, the closest I'd ever gotten to one was when I was a hostess at a Denny's for a few months 40 years ago. I was certainly not invited into that busy kitchen but had caught glimpses of the chaos. Fortunately, for my first year as manager at Luccock, we had a chef, Terri, and her husband, Russ, a skilled line cook, on staff, so I didn't really have to overthink things like ordering food or exactly how much time it takes to cook bacon for 200 guests. It just happened under their watchful eye.

As I often do, I did see ways to make things more efficient, cleaner, and less labor-intensive at Luccock, mainly in the dish pit. My goal was to have the happiest, cleanest dish pit in the state. Each inspector who tours here seem to feel I have hit the mark, as laughter generally fills the air and the floors are cleaned nightly, which I assumed happened in kitchens everywhere, but apparently I am sadly mistaken.

While washing dishes and helping to serve food, I learned that it is a hell of a lot of work to be in a kitchen. It is hot. Damn hot. And it is endless. When breakfast is over, lunch begins, and dinner is not far behind. Our kitchen staff keeps their heads down and plows forward day after day, smiling shyly when campers want to recognize them for a job well done.

One day, after chopping, oh, I don't know, about 80 heads of cauliflower for dinner, many of which I knew would end up in the garbage cans, I rubbed my sore back and applied yet another Band-Aid to my lacerated fingers. I thought I could chop the way they do on TV if I just tried hard enough. That theory turned out to be a pipe dream. That is when Terri said one of the wisest things I have ever heard. It was even kind of under her breath, which makes it uber suitable for a book about Quiet Leadership.

She said, "You hurt yourself in the kitchen only until you decide to stop hurting yourself in the kitchen." I stopped, took a step back, and asked her to explain what she knew from years behind a stove. She told me that people often ignore systems, processes, and their own signals in a mad dash to complete the task or prove that they know better than those who mentor them. (Like my manic cauliflower chopping technique!)

Teri said once you decide you'd like to end your shift without Band-Aids and Tylenol, you take more care, take more breaks, and actually take time to accomplish the task without causing yourself pain. Terri lived with several ailments, and walked with a cane that summer but insisted that she still felt alive at the end of the day because she'd decided to stop causing herself pain in the kitchen.

I am sure that by now you have thought of the deeper implications here, this transfer of wisdom to every job, every relationship, every choice you make for yourself and your life.

You hurt yourself only until you decide to stop hurting yourself.

It is true in the kitchen. It is true in the warehouse, on the job site, sitting hunched at a computer. It is also true in relationships that are wrong, and exercise and eating habits that do more harm than good. *You hurt yourself only until you decide to stop hurting yourself.*

There is a day when you decide that you, the person doing the work, is just as important as the work. That you, the person with so much to give, is worthy of a recipient who cares about you as much as you do about them. As leaders, as humans who want the best for those we hire, mentor, and lead throughout the day, there should also be a sense of release here, a weight we can take off our shoulders.

As leaders we can provide the right tools, say the right words, cast a vision of what can be, if only they want to look at it as we do. Still, we cannot do the work for them, we cannot erase the pain, stop the madness, the self-inflicted pain, or even—and sometimes this is the most brutal truth—guarantee the success, until they decide to stop hurting themselves, whether in the kitchen or the boardroom.

And that is what I learned, quietly, while doing kitchen duty in a space I never expected to occupy but can't imagine leaving.

Quiet Leadership

PART THREE   LEADING A COMMUNITY, QUIETLY

...serving your community in the best way you know will give you satisfaction like no other.

When I first gathered a group to fight a public injustice, my dad and several others told me not to. They said things like "they" will take care of it, not to poke a bear, let sleeping dogs lie, and that I didn't know what I was doing or getting into as I forged ahead. And they were right, but only about the last statement. I didn't know what I was getting into or how to do it, but I did it anyway. And in the end, we won.

At a public hearing, I discovered that there was a toxic dump in our neighborhood. I attended the meeting to argue that our streets and schools didn't have room for a new subdivision of 100 houses, an age-old, ineffective argument. During the testimony, we learned there were unbelievable levels of PCPs in the ground, and the recommendation was to ignore the implications and cover them up with a layer of dirt. I didn't know anything about PCPs, but this didn't sound right, so I started asking questions. Once I had a mitt full of facts and figures, I gathered people in the know and people with valid concerns about the outcome. And we quickly but quietly rolled into fixing the problem because from what we gathered "they" surely weren't going to do it correctly. In the end, without once raising my voice but after several threats to shoot out my windows, the site became a Superfund Cleanup site and eventually a pristine neighborhood park with 50 houses surrounding it.

During that fight, called the Neighborhood Alliance, I learned what I still believe works.

Gather the facts. Not the talking points, the rallying cries, or the political agendas, just the facts. Then look at them objectively. If you don't understand them, as I didn't, move to step two.

Gather the people. Start with people who know more than you. Add in dissenting opinions because often they have a few good points, and if you work with them as much as possible, they will reciprocate and work *with* you. (This is paramount to solving big problems, working together with a variety of opinions.) Then add in those affected by the problem and those who can fix the problem. Gather people who remain calm and objective but are also passionate about the outcome. I've tried working with the hotheads, hoping their passion would ignite results, but more often than not that has derailed the entire process. Thus my penchant for Quiet Leadership.

Remain calm but steady. Do not release the steady pressure of achieving your goal; stay involved from beginning to end because if the leader lets off the accelerator, all forward motion will stop. Calmly talk to the decision-makers, befriend the media, and give space for your adversaries to state their cases respectfully. The key to success is always to remain calm and steady. Any deviation will cause havoc to the process. During my first visit with the press in the dumpsite, my tears made the newsreels at every turn. They made me look emotional and unhinged. I vowed never to cry on camera or in a meeting again. Calm, steady strength, that's what wins for your community.

Be magnanimous in victory. I joke that I can out-humble anyone, which is, of course, antithetical to being humble. When you win the battle, when the opposing side tosses in the towel, allow them to walk away with their heads held high. Grace bestowed is always grace returned. If you treat your win as a moment of humble gratitude, you will lead other battles, and your antagonists might become your allies.

Do it again. It is our role as leaders to lead. I abhor armchair quarterbacks and backroom whiners. If there is a problem, and if you can help fix it, then help fix it. Do not waste your life carping about the problems, then cut out the solutions. Help. If you're a leader, you do not have to take on every project, especially as *the leader*, but your passion and voice will be needed time and again. Allow space to do it again.

Your community—whether that's a church council, a little league team, or an entire city—will probably look to you to be a problem solver at some point. It can be challenging to step into a public role, but it is amazingly gratifying. There is no need to take on every problem, and there is no need to wear yourself out fighting battles that are not part of your day-to-day mission. Enough is enough.

Say no when it is prudent, but say yes when your heart can't let you say no. When you step forward, trying to fix what is broken, others will also step forward. Your confidence will grow, as will your reputation, and the lessons you learn while leading a community will make you a better leader for your other teams as well.

And, my Quiet Leader, serving your community in the best way you know will give you satisfaction like no other. I talk about this in the next chapter, "Two Drunks and a Mayor." When I worry that I have not done enough for the world, when I say no to a project that cannot gain my whole heart, I look to our I'll Help community and feel the satisfaction of a job well done, a project that matters, and I relax into the peace of having done what I can, for now. You deserve that feeling.

If you look around the room, around the community you are building, and everyone gets along, has the same thoughts, goes about things in exactly the same way, your community is going to fail. No one will trust the process, the goals, or the outcome because the pool is too tidy, too small, and there is no splash of excitement as people debate the next move.

TWO DRUNKS AND A MAYOR

I am going to tell you the secret to building a strong community because as a leader, that's what you get to do, build community. It might be a city, it might be a club, a congregation, or more likely a work team, but over and over, as you move along your leadership path, you will need to know how to build a community. As you know, the base of community building is easy; shared interests in space or mission, a similar commitment to solving a problem, coming together to commune, build, or enjoy the same thing. A community can grow out of many and any common situations or shared experiences.

The more challenging part is building trust in that community.

Trust that this is the right place, time, and way for the community to do things. Trust that the leader has the vision, and the workers have the guts and the tools to build the community. Trust that if you do this, whatever it is you are doing together, it will help more than it will hurt; it will thrive and not fail. There is a myriad of ways to build trust and just as many ways to break it. But what I know, after building communities of all shapes and sizes for purposes of solving the problems created

180

by a toxic dump in our neighborhood to an online community of people moving towards their Nexts, is this:

Building your community with clones of you doesn't work.

Sure, you are a fine human, a quality leader, a great friend, spouse, and even child to your parents, but good gosh and golly, if your whole community looks like you, no one is going to have enough trust in it to stop for a visit.

You see, to be effective, a community needs two drunks and a mayor. It requires a pastor and a vixen, an artist and an accountant. A community needs a jester, a doctor, a liar, and a police officer. It requires a 10-year-old and an 80-year-old, and it needs one full-on asshole and one of the nicest people you are ever going to meet.

If you look around the room, around the community you are building, and everyone gets along, has the same thoughts, goes about things in exactly the same way, your community is going to fail. No one will trust the process, the goals, or the outcome because the pool is too tidy, too small, and there is no splash of excitement as people debate the next move.

In a time when we curate our music, our news, and our neighborhoods, it is often scary to walk into the chaos of a community built on differences. Still, I promise you this, once you get past that fear, the reward is enlightened, invigorated growth. The conversations are more animated, the debates more intense. There are differences to hear, ideas to truly debate, and minds to change. The beauty of it all is when the mind that is changed is yours. That is a beautiful day in a community when you, as a leader, can listen, ask, discern, consider, and then change your mind to agree with someone who appears to be the exact opposite of you.

It takes trust to build those conversations, and grace to listen when you want to speak. It takes power to hold your tongue until it is your turn to talk and manners to speak in a way that allows others to hold onto their differences while considering yours. As a leader, that is what you must do. Ask others to share your vision, and walk your path while still holding onto the beliefs, ideals, and knowledge that makes them different from you.

Sometimes the best, loudest thing you can say or do is to sit and listen quietly, to watch as the conversations unfold, appreciate the new perspectives, and repeat back the things that seem odd to you, asking for clarification. When you quietly give space to new ways of thinking, of being, your community bonds and begins to move together, even if kindred is not in their makeup.

Quiet Leadership allows you to gather people who don't see eye to eye with you and listen to them instead of demanding their obedience. Quiet Leadership allows you the grace to discover if someone else is right or if their way of thinking helps you to solidify yours. Quiet Leadership gives you the power, the grace even, to lead in a way that encourages healthy debate, and welcomes needed change without using bullhorns or force. Quiet Leadership will help you change the things you do not like, right the wrongs, and fix the glaring problems with a community at your side, one that looks nothing like you and makes you all the stronger because of that fact.

Be a Quiet Leader, one who is leading the most awkward-looking community you have ever seen, and you can move that mountain you have been trying to climb.

I cannot talk about building community and not tell this story.

Jennifer Owen, a lawyer, nonprofit leader, community council person, and someone I admire greatly, took me to lunch. She told me about the problems with the child welfare system in our town, specifically for foster children. The facts she laid out in front of me were shocking, mainly because I had my middle-class, everything-is-fine glasses on most of the time. I knew we had homelessness, but I didn't know one of our elementary schools consists of 30% homeless students. I knew our town of 100,000 had foster children, but I didn't think we had as many as Cincinnati, a city of 1,754,000. Clearly, something had to be done.

So we asked Jennifer Reiser, the COO of our Chamber of Commerce, to help us assemble a group of businesspeople and college students (we invited them because they—lovingly—know everything.) We called the event Figure It Out. For several hours we educated each other on what was actually happening in our town and puzzled out how we could have an impact. We came up with several ideas, the best of which was a community on Facebook called "I'll Help" – Billings. We first invited foster parents to this page, but eventually, as helpers came on faster than those needing help, anyone in our community who needed help was welcomed.

The idea was simple; if I don't have the bandwidth to foster, I can certainly pick up diapers for someone who does. I could sort of wrap my arms around them and support these parents as they did what I couldn't, but what needed to be done, just the same.

The page blew up. We added three helpers for every one who needed help, and no foster need went unmet. Within two years, we had over 7000 members and dozens of posts each day.

The page has become not just a place for people to get help, but a place where people share knowledge of the system and where and when support is available. Every week, in a beautiful turn of events, we see someone who reached out for help now offering to help. Sometimes it is not much, but they give as openly as they were given to when they asked. We have seen people give one another formula, clothing, furniture, cars, rides, and even found people housing. Sometimes they take each other dinner, and sometimes helpers just give members space to tell their stories.

Importantly, and much rawer, people living on the edge often do tell their stories, sometimes in great detail; and it shocks people like me who are living a totally different kind of life, one without trauma, without tragic events happening regularly. And in doing so, they have opened the eyes of my business friends and many policymakers. Our community knows we can make better, kinder decisions, because we see the results of those decisions in real time. We can also, now understand how sometimes simply keeping an appointment with someone who is going to help you is the hardest thing in the world to do.

This community looks like the community I've described in this chapter: built of drunks and pastors, socialites and homeless, young and old. And each and every day the community gives selflessly of both their needs and their gifts, their pain and their solutions.

It is a community I am very proud to be associated with and an example of how diverse people can quietly offer words as simple as "I'll Help" and change the world because of them.

This page, this vibrant pain and hope-filled community has shown me, in real-time, that asking for help is often the hardest thing you can do, and helping is the kindest thing you can do. I also recognize stingy givers and sticky takers from a distance and wish neither of them was part of life, but here we are. Communities need all kinds of people, even one devoted to helping foster children.

Imagine what those closest to us have to say if we are ready to listen without telling them what we think first.

TALKING TO STRANGERS

We stepped through the doors of a building that was a café, bar, gas station, hotel, and yes, even the proprietor's home, as well as the town post office somewhere north of Dawson Creek, British Columbia, and south of the Alaskan border. My husband, ever careful in, well, any situation, but especially ones that seem a bit curious, grabbed my hand and said, very clearly, and under his breath. We want to know NOTHING, Karen; don't ask one question.

Are you kidding? How could I not ask even one question? I mean, really, how did they decide this was the place they wanted to live? How many weary winter travelers stop by on any given day; were the cinnamon rolls, which looked a little dusty, edible; did the barking dog, who was leaping at us while chained up near the door, bite anyone; did they have a bathroom, which is really what I needed…? NO questions!? Come on, man, not even one?

Fine.

I found the bathroom, and Paul bought a cinnamon roll, which, as it turns out, was delicious, and we really should have bought a dozen. And there I was without the recipe I could have gotten had I asked one question. But no, the mister wanted to give them their space as they seemed like people who liked their space, which is why they were proprietors and occupants of the only building on this 400-mile stretch of lonely road called the AlCan. I gave them their space, but I didn't like it.

I didn't like it, because I like people.

I like that they are where I am, whether at a store or in line for a concert. I like that they have skills I don't. I like people who are doing things I wish I knew how to do, and I like people who are oh so different than me. I want people to know I like their new shoes, the flowers they bought at the grocery, and that their child is the cutest child I have ever seen because everyone deserves a compliment. I like them to know that when they hand me my receipt, they are worth looking in the eye and genuinely thanking. Mostly, I like people because people have stories.

And I like to know those stories. But sometimes, the stories come with a little bit too much information. Which is what my husband was afraid of at the cobbled-together, multipurpose building in Canada, that they might tell me more than I wanted to know, or worse, wonder who I was and why I wanted to know what was in the back room. At the next stop on the AlCan I overruled his objection, asked a question, and learned things I didn't actually *want* to know while he snickered in the truck.

Yes, I talk to strangers. I talk to people I probably shouldn't, and I talk to people who probably wish I wasn't talking to them, but I try to be very careful about that! I start the conversations slowly, with a compliment or a smile, and then I ask a question, which I have perfected as a coach but is a skill I learned from my dad. When I was old enough to listen to him (finally), he taught me that if you asked three questions before you started yammering (his word, not mine), that conversation would be much richer, full of ideas and learning.

I've taken that advice and built a business around it, but more importantly, I created a library of stories I would never have known had I not asked questions of strangers. One of my favorite "stranger" stories has become a life-long friend, a man whose pants were too short to go with his cowboy boots but who bought my coffee because he wanted to tell me about his adventures in space. Yes, an astronaut, but not the NASA kind, the tourist kind, who paid the Russians to take him for a ride.

Three other times I met men on planes, sitting in first class, where if you know what you are doing (and I clearly don't as my seat is usually a bump, not a purchase), you sit quietly with your headset on, looking forward. Anyway, three different men told me tear-filled stories about their grandmothers. They told me about these women who loved them unconditionally and took the time to listen to them. One told the story of how he and his grandma were so wrapped up in conversation that she failed to notice she was driving on a newly paved road, and by the time she realized what she had done, the tires were caked with tar, rubbing the fenders, and the car was a disaster. Those two were banned from unsupervised car rides for a long time, something that made him very proud. The rest of the story was that he was on his way to buy her a new car, simply because he could, and that made him proud, too.

Grandmas. We all know they are essential, but did you know they are so very important that when given a willing ear, they will be the story that flows? That is both humbling and an ideal to live up to as a grandparent.

I think the idea of being a willing ear is most important, and not just to grandchildren. Complete strangers will tell you how they made their fortune, how they lost their spouse, and why they became the World Hacky Sack Champion (that really is a thing; I met him flying into Billings, neither of us in first class) if you just provide a willing ear. Imagine what those closest to us have to say if we are ready to listen without telling them what we think first.

In the time before, as my friend Tina Roberts calls the days before Covid, it was easy to start a conversation. No masks to hide a smile or a smirk, never caring about a pesky little germ. I am looking forward to those days again. I promise, when they arrive, to be on my very best behavior. Because right now, someone is telling a story about how a young woman (it was very long ago, and I was very naïve), pantomimed, with great exaggeration, while slowly and clearly saying, "Do. You. Want.

My. Pretzels?" to which the woman of the group replied, "No thanks, and we speak English."

That didn't break the ice, which would be the perfect way to end this chapter. What it did teach me was to pay better attention and to lean in when the moment was just right, to ask another question, and to let people know that they matter and that their story does too.

This chapter was originally published in Yellowstone Valley Woman *magazine, I think this story is the beauty of Quiet Leadership, leaning in, letting people know they matter, in both expected and unexpected places. Ask a few questions. Ask a few more. Listen. Lead. Quietly.*

Quiet Leadership

Never disobey your parents.

Never disobey your teachers.

Never break the law.

~Bob Cox Wisdom

FLY-FISHING

Since writing *Seasoned,* the story of my husband's accident called The Fall with Jesus, and subsequent miracles, I have thought about older men and their lifelong hobbies and treasured memories. I have looked for old men passing down traditions and children looking up to those men in awe of their wisdom. (Be aware, sometimes awe looks like boredom.) If you've read *Seasoned,* you know that I was sure Paul had a loving grandfather teach him to fly-fish by reciting, "10 and 2, present the fly to the fish as if it is a gift, 10 and 2." (Imagine standing with your shoulder sideways to a clockface—you move your fly rod from 10:00 to 2:00 for a perfect cast.)

That was not the case. Paul learned to fly-fish on his own as a teen, and seldom has he been without a fly rod since.

Standing in the water gives Paul clarity, freedom from my helpful suggestions of household chores to complete, and a rhythm to his life and friendships. 10 and 2, 10 and 2, feel the rhythm of the riffles, watch the fly skim along on the surface of the water. 10 and 2, set the hook, release the fish with a smile and gratitude. Then back to 10 and 2.

Today? Well, today, I saw a child smile and knew that someday he would be an old man, telling the story of how his grandfather taught him to fly-fish, how 10 and 2 calms him and gives him clarity. How standing in the water gives him a sense of being grounded, at one with nature, and reminds him of two old men who gave him a gift to build a life around.

Paul's friend Bob Cox, who is a legend for teaching children all over our community how to tie flies, how to fish, and how to behave, built a fly rod for our grandson, Ezra. Ezra, one of the most well-mannered children I have ever known, was handed the rod to examine, and he did a brilliant job of feigning interest. While examining it, he saw his name inscribed on the side of the rod and his interest turned into a satisfied smile.

Later he said, "I cried a little."

"Why?"

"Because of all the time that went into this gift."

Truth be told, we all cried a little—well, except Bob. Bob was his stoic and energetic self. He spent 40 hours building this rod. He chose just the right guides, used thread that would sparkle as the sunlight bounced off the water, and created a handle that "feels good in my hand," according to Ezra. Bob waited, like all adults, to give a legacy to a child, with great anticipation of this gifting, and was not disappointed by the reaction.

After a lifetime of watching people, I know now that Bob gave Ezra more than a rod, more than a hobby, and he gave him someone to idolize.

With our whole family assembled, drinking coffee, we watched as Bob told Ezra both life and fish stories and left him with three rules for life:

Never disobey your parents, because they buy your clothes, food, and toys. They deserve respect.

 Never disobey your teachers, because someday you will want to go back and hug them for the lessons they have taught you.

Never break the law, because you cannot enjoy fishing or the other wonderful things this life offers you if you break the law.

Then he told Ezra he could do anything he wanted, be anyone he wanted, and that life is his for the taking. Ezra, who was no longer feigning awe, listened, nodded his head, and smiled the kindest smile I have ever seen. Only ten years old, he knew that this moment was not just for him. Ezra knew it was for Bob, and Nick, his dad, and his grandpa, the man we call Seasoned.

Ezra is a treasured only grandchild, and with that role comes many a duty, like too many gifts at Christmas, too many head pats, and heaps of lessons we hope to pass down, because that is what the old folks do, pass down lessons, and hopes, and traditions we hope will last a lifetime.

This fly rod comes with promises of times by a creek, flies to be tied, and stories to be heard again, and again and again. Stories he will remember when he is an old man, standing in the water saying 10 and 2, 10 and 2.

I hope the Quiet Leadership lessons that Ezra carries through life include this one, the passing down of wisdom and tradition. And I hope that you, Quiet Leader, take time to share what you love, what you know, or what you think are the three most important lessons in life with a child you have never met before, or like Bob, a whole community of children. They deserve the chance to hold you in awe, even if a fly rod is not involved, because you know things that will carry them far.

Quiet Leadership

It is the people who have been batted around by life who often solve the most challenging problems. The nibbled and crumpled sheet of paper gives credence to the entire project.

GRASSHOPPER NIBBLES

Like so many middle-class, middle-aged Americans, Barb Cromwell grew up on a diet of Jell-O molds, simple carbohydrate snacks, and iceberg lettuce salad. Her mom lovingly prepared the foods, with a fantastic ability to feed four or ten people, without ever breaking a sweat, as guests often stopped by right at dinner time.

When Barb's children came along, their digestive systems required more care, more thought, hours of worry, and many sleepless nights. Determined to end their suffering, Barb searched for the best food choices. These choices included minimal ingredients, actual local foods raised lovingly by organic farmers, and less mainstream, more nutritious ingredients. The trouble was, while these foods helped her kids to thrive, they were not readily available in her hometown of Rapid City, South Dakota. Barb had to seek out small farmers and ranchers for the best of the best, foods that weren't in the mega groceries, but instead raised with a passionate commitment to nutrition over photographic qualities. Barb's compassionate spirit drove her to help solve the problem of sourcing these foods because she knew this need for nutrients didn't affect only her family but many others, which led her to lead the local farmer's market.

And by leading, I don't mean she simply invited farmers and consumers to the same space simultaneously. She researched the best practices and those who followed them, asking only the best to showcase their crops. She championed farmers who had helped her solve her family's health problems and educated consumers on what it means to eat genuinely organic foods. (Worms in your corn and grasshopper nibbles in your salad make Barb happy!) And as often happens, while solving one problem, you discover another, so Barb became a leader of the farm-to-table movement, a trusted resource with the passion for feeding the masses well, working with state and local officials to fill her market with nutrient providers and grateful buyers.

But, as leaders often find, the masses don't always know what is good for them. The masses usually follow the reset of the masses, right off the cliff, even if you stand in front of them and say, "That's not working!"

According to Barb, one of the many things not working is an expectation of perfection in whole foods. Perfection, at least in crops, is hard to attain. Sure, your romaine lettuce fits neatly, five to a bag, for your Costco purchase, but at what cost?

When a small-time farmer grows a crop, they plan, they dig, they sow, they watch and worry, they cheer the breakthrough seedlings, and they even welcome the peskiest of bugs into the process because the pesky bugs know a thing or two about agriculture that you and I don't. Those bugs often eliminate other bugs that can ruin a farmer's dreams of a crisp and delicious harvest with one afternoon snack. Often this snack does not eat the crop down to the ground; it is simply a nibble here and bite there, and the bugs hop along to the next tasty-looking leaf to do the same, marring perfection one nibble at a time.

What Barb fights against, what she feels is one of her biggest challenges, is our inability to look past the nibble to the nutrition in the rest of the leaf or crop. Buyers see the grasshopper nibble and pass on the truckload of lettuce. Hours of a farmer's work and hope that went into the crop are negated with a shake of the head.

As leaders, I would contend that we often do this with our people and their projects.

We see the grasshopper nibbles, the chinks in the armor, and worry that the person or the project is not enough. That the nibble created a fault, and the fault could mean ruin. Seldom is this true. It is the people who have been batted around by life who often solve the most challenging problems. The nibbled and crumpled sheet of paper often gives credence to the entire project.

As leaders, we need to look past the grasshopper nibbles and accept that grasshoppers only nibble on the best lettuce. They look for the juiciest, the most promising morsels, and when they find it, they dig in and ask for more.

You can do that too. Look for the nibbles, the organic imperfections, and then take a big bite of potential for greatness.

Yes, there is work getting done, wrongs that are being righted, and problems that are being fixed every day. It is being done by quiet people, people who believe that doing something is better than doing nothing and that even if they don't know exactly what needs to be done, they know something needs to be done, and so they start with the smallest action, something they can handle, and they do that. These small actions, built one on top of the other, make all the difference to our world.

STAND UP. SIT DOWN. MAKE IT RIGHT.

We have been together long enough now that I'm sure I can be brutally honest with you.

I have no time for carpers, whiners, or problem pointer outers with no plan to fix a damn thing. I don't care which way you vote; I don't care how much education or money or how many opinions you have. What I do care about is that you either sit down, stand up, get involved in trying to make it right, or be quiet while the rest of us go to work fixing the problems in our world.

You know by now that I am not about the riot, I am not about the finger-pointing or the credit for a well done, I am, however, all about doing *something*. If you tell me you believe in world peace and even demand it, you better do something for world peace. Stand up and make a change, or sit down and write a letter. If you tell me you can't believe that we allow working families to sleep in homes without beds, then you better be gathering beds. If you don't at least try to make it right, I won't fully listen as you carp about a community problem.

Yes, I am fired up and passionate about this. I am getting old, and so are you (sorry if you weren't aware), and there is a lot of shit that needs fixing, and it is not being fixed by people who are standing on the sidelines carping as other people work.

Yes, there is work getting done, wrongs that are being righted, and problems that are being fixed every day. It is being done by quiet people, people who believe that doing something is better than doing nothing and that even if they don't know *exactly* what needs to be done, they know *something* needs to be done, and so they start with the smallest action, something they can handle, and they do that. These small actions, built one on top of the other, make all the difference to our world. The small movements, the ones the TV cameras overlook, give me hope for tomorrow; those actions are pure love and dedication to helping.

Every day, you have seen problems that need to be fixed (well, if you were looking), and more than once, you have said somebody should do something. Well, you are somebody and today is your day. Put down the book, stand behind a leader, or sit down and write a letter. Follow those who need help fixing a problem, or ask people to follow you as you forge a new path to a better tomorrow. You won't do it wrong. You may make a mistake, but doing something is never wrong.

Please, for the love of all that is right in this world, don't ignore a problem you can help fix. You will sleep better at night and learn to be a better leader by doing something. You will make a difference for your community, and for our world, if you get out there quietly and do something.

Stand up. Sit down. Make it right.

Quiet Leader, you have a voice. It may be a voice for change, or it may be a voice for championing change makers. Whatever it is, I hope you are using it well and carefully.

GIVING VOICE TO A COMMUNITY

The best Quiet Leaders know that people will do what you celebrate. They also know that as leaders, they have a responsibility to do what they can to improve their community, whether that's a small group of like-minded individuals or an entire city. Since that is true, it stands to reason that the best way to improve a community is to use whatever you have as a stage and loudly and proudly celebrate the people and the actions you would like to see repeated. Your voice is magnified, which is essential when leading a community, and your goals are easier to achieve if you do this well.

Julie Koerber does it well. Very well. The owner and publisher of *Yellowstone Valley Woman* magazine, Julie and her team have high ideals for what they will publish, thus celebrating in the pages of their magazine. They look for women who are doing the right things, the hard things, and more often than not, the unsung things to improve the community they serve. These women are typically standing outside of the spotlight, working long hours, leading teams of like-minded people, and they are often relatively unknown until Julie puts them on the cover of *YVW*.

This magazine, the premier magazine for our region, has a reputation for quality stories, quality pictures, and advertisers dedicated to doing good works in the community. It is noteworthy when a woman is featured on the cover or in a story. Being featured gives these women a boost, not just personally but professionally. Their businesses often see a nice bump in opportunities, and their causes get a much-needed spotlight from the publicity.

Because of these facts, Julie and her team have learned how to suss out the best stories, tell them well, and as a result, increase the reach of the women who matter. It is an incredible way to build a more positive, helpful community, which is what happens with each issue. Often, regional and area magazines zero in on fluff pieces featuring only the beautiful, only the happy, only the easiest ways to make their readers smile. *YVW* decided they would be more than fluff. They have tackled such things as addiction, foster children aging out of the system, and the disappearance and silencing of Native women. The stories are heartfelt but factual, a tribute to Julie's days as a hard-hitting news journalist. Not shying away from the pain makes the stories of joy and comfort all the more enjoyable.

Being a Quiet Leader often means tackling complicated problems. Julie shows us that sometimes the best Quiet Leaders tackle not just one but dozens of complex problems by celebrating the leaders who are leading the charges for change and uncovering the problems that need to be addressed.

Quiet Leader, you have a voice. It may be a voice for change, or it may be a voice for championing change makers. Whatever it is, I hope you are using it well and carefully. You don't have to yell, and you don't have to toss grenades, but, as someone with skills and passion, you would be wasting your voice if you didn't use it to make the world a better place, which is exactly what Julie and her team do with every issue.

...but if other people like to tap you on the shoulder and hand you their bag of shit, you have the power to stop letting it stick to you. Not only do you have the power, but you also have an obligation to stop carrying it around.

BULLSHIT

There was a time when I was the queen of LinkedIn. I had a big following, a lot of momentum, and was loving the ride. Mind you, I didn't have a million followers, like some, but those I did have were engaged, and we were making things happen. Every day I would have get-to-know-you calls, some leading to business, some leading to boredom. And then I had a 15-minute get-to-know-you call with Elizabeth Tuckwell, owner of the Art of Wellness. We were both using creativity in our businesses and knew we were destined to be friends, so we scheduled another hour-long call. As we started talking, I knew we should have scheduled a day. My mind was blown.

Elizabeth started doing an intuitive reading for me, something I didn't expect, she told me things she could see in my house. She was in Chicago, and I was in Billings, mind you, and this was in the days before Zoom. She also knew exactly how I was feeling about life—more than I even did. I was experiencing a time of questioning, of trying to figure life out, of meditating, praying, pacing, and, when the mood hit, yelling at God for not giving me the answer I sought by Thursday at 3:00 p.m. Paul wasn't home, and I didn't have the guts to go camping alone, so I had spent the night before sleeping in the backyard, under the stars, hoping a change of pace, a few hours under the dark sky, would clear my mind. In a way it did, and in the middle of the night, I got up and scribbled some decisions on the chalkboard in our back entry.

Elizabeth described that chalkboard to me, where it was placed, what color it was, and that it had some sort of scribbling on it. Okay, so my handwriting, done with a tiny piece of chalk in the dark, isn't that great. To be fair, a Montblanc pen at noon doesn't improve it all that much. To say she had my full attention is to understate how much I needed the lifeline she was throwing me. She knew me, she could see me, and she cared enough to be straight with me.

As we talked she said, "You need to stop letting other people's bullshit get stuck to you. You take on everyone's problems, worries, fears, and anger, and it has worn you out. Their bullshit is weighing you down, and soon you won't be able to do what you need to do for the world, inspiring it with your process and your words." I cried.

I knew she was right. So very right.

We talked about eliminating my stickiness and ridding myself of the stink. When we got off the phone, I cleaned my house from top to bottom, dropping salt on rugs and in corners, as Elizabeth suggested, and opened the windows to the east so the evil spirits could escape. Now this might sound kooky to you, and it did to me, but I did it anyway. My mother-in-law was a faith healer, and I've seen some things....

Then I escaped. I went to a cabin in the mountains to meditate, heal, and hear *myself* for a change. Getting ready, I practiced something I think we should all do from time to time: saying yes to myself. I packed only clothes I loved to wear and pens and paper I loved to touch and use to create. When I stopped at the grocery for supplies, no food was off-limits; I could eat whatever I wanted. I seemed to choose only the most flavorful and healthiest foods with that freedom. I wondered why I didn't behave like that all of the time. It felt beautiful and freeing, this act of saying yes.

I spent the weekend meditating, walking a makeshift labyrinth counterclockwise, and napping. Oh, the napping, long decadent naps like I'd never had before. I can still feel the calm as I think of those naps. Before it was time to leave, I sat on the grass, looking at the mountains. I was outside a small chapel, with a cross framed by an azure sky. The grass was soft and green, so I laid down to soak in all of the majesties of the moment. Elizabeth had said there was something in my life that I had let get obscured and overgrown, like an unkempt woodland. While walking the labyrinth, I noticed a weathered cross standing in front of an unkempt forest, and I knew, with a clarity I hadn't felt in a long time, that my faith was what I was ignoring. I had let life grow over it, and I needed it back. Later, lying in the grass, looking at that cross, I knew my faith would carry me through whatever changes were ahead of me.

Soon, I rolled over, ready to go home, and there, right under my face, was, I kid you not, a dried-up pile of bullshit. I live in Montana so these things happen, but now? How could this not be a sign? My instinct was to get away from it as fast as possible, but I stopped for a moment and really looked at that pile of bullshit. Deep down on a cellular level, I knew that I did not want to take that home with me and that I would never again let other people's (or a bull's) crap attach to my life. I was free.

When I got home, I cleaned the house again, vacuuming salt from the rugs and corners, preparing this space to serve my highest ideals. I showered, meditated, and had a short call with Paul, who was in Alaska working and hanging out with a friend. All was well, so I went to bed, comfortable that my life was bullshit free.

At midnight, the phone rang. Paul had taken a fall, a catastrophic fall, actually, and it is a miracle he lived through it. I was on a plane a couple of hours later and by his side as soon as I took a shower and changed clothes to scrub off any germs (bullshit?) I picked up on the plane. We call his fall the fall with Jesus, and I wrote about it in my book *Seasoned.* All that is important here, for Quiet Leadership, is this.

I was ready.

I could handle any and all of the work, the pain, the horrid financial fallout this brought into our lives. None of it stuck to me. I worked through it, looked past it, and never let the stink of disappointment, resentment, and unmitigated bullshit stick to me. It was the most challenging time in our lives, but it was so full of beauty, daily miracles, miracles I was ready to receive because I had cleaned my house, my soul, and my communication channels with God. All of it was unmarred by a propensity of stickiness for other people's bullshit.

So, leader, you might not need to pour salt in the corners, you might not need to put your nose inches from a dung pile in order to grow forward, but if other people like to tap you on the shoulder and hand you their bag of shit, you have the power to stop letting it stick to you. Not only do you have the power, but you also have an obligation to stop carrying it around. While you are carrying the stinking load, you are so weighed down that you can't celebrate the best of life or your people.

How do you do this? How do you not pick up the bag or let unwanted energy stick to you? Some say you should meditate and surround yourself with white light before every interaction; others ask God for protection. My mother-in-law wore an Inuit Soul Catcher Ring. The legend says the hole in the ring would hold the healer's soul while they did their work, and it would be there, in perfect order, when they were through.

Counseling is a good choice, and so is asking yourself what you have let get overgrown and are ignoring. Is it your faith, your health, your hobbies, that give you pleasure? Take heed and practice them again.

How do I remain bullshit-free? Well, I try to do many of those things, and I say yes to myself more now. Yes to a good meal, a nap, a day away from the chaos. I also ask myself, during most interactions, if I want what they are throwing to get stuck to me. If not, I determine how I can help them and what I will take away as the moment ends.

When the bullshit is flying, I often ask people what they would like me to do with it. Do they want commiseration or counsel? Do they want to be heard or helped? What were they hoping for by sharing this with me? And you know what? That last question is never answered with, "Well, I want to stick this crap on your back so I can weigh you down, too."

It is your job as a leader to carry the torch, take water to your followers, and show up, day after day, for the work you get to do for the world.

It is not your job, Quiet Leader, to carry any bullshit. Wipe it off now, and be careful where you step going forward. Bullshit is everywhere, but so is beauty, hope, and miracles. I know because I look for and find them every single day, in every single moment.

You can do that too.

Quietly.

And also with gusto, because pointing out the joy to others just might help them to get out from under the bullshit that is stuck to them.

And that is what I learned from a remarkable woman during one phone call. I sure am glad I said yes to that!

Still, I believe in God. I have seen too many miraculous moments not to. I have felt comfort, guidance, and the contentment that comes from faith in a higher power.

I believe in God.

I don't often say that out loud because I like for everyone to think that I vote as they vote, I eat as they eat, and I pray as they pray.

It's not because I am not strong in my convictions; it is because I would rather discuss things—big ideas, strong values— without the overshadowing of someone trying to convince me I am wrong and they are right. I don't want to be *convinced*, and I don't want others to fear I will spend our precious time together forcing my ideas on them, either. And, frankly, it is better for business if I can meld with the group without the cloud of my personal opinions ruling the event.

I also believe in the universe, the bluebird of happiness, and the power of free-will and self reliance. Still, I believe in God. I have seen too many miraculous moments not to. I have felt comfort, guidance, and the contentment that comes from faith in a higher power, but there are still days when God seems so far away that I can run down the path of the agnostic, questioning and doubting every single thing about a higher deity.

And, frankly, I am not convinced that there is only one way to find God, only one true way to act or believe or walk the path of being a human. I love a reverent Catholic Mass, the fluttering of

Buddhist prayer flags, a powerful Pentecostal choir, and the fact that Lutherans don't clap in church. I love these things because I love the faces of those drawn to *their* form of faith, no matter what it is. The smile of a prayer well said, the peace of knowing, the joy of worship, is the most beautiful look you will see on our fellow humans. I also believe faith is a private matter, like arguments with your spouse and morning breath; some things don't need to be blasted to the masses.

So, it surprised me, as much as it did anyone, to find me Friday after Friday standing on the very public corner called Sky Point, in Billings, Montana, praying with a group of civic and business leaders for our city. We stood there in rain, snow, and sunshine. We stood there quietly, timidly, peacefully, and sometimes boldly praying for our city, almost shyly at first. We stood there because we were scared, tired, and looking for hope in a time full of Covid chaos and social unrest. I went because one of the people I respected most, Steve Arveschoug, executive director of Big Sky EDA, was leading the cause, and when Steve invites me to an event, I always try to say yes.

We met a few minutes before 8:00 a.m. so we could make eight o'clock meetings. Our time together quickly fell into a rhythm. Brief hellos, everyone in the circle offering their words of prayer, and then quick good-byes as we dashed back to our duties.

As the prayers were offered, we had tiny glimpses into one another's lives and businesses, but this was not time for networking or relationship building. This gathering was pure;

this was simple, this was quiet, this was a group of believers standing together, asking for and being thankful for the gifts of faith, hope, and charity for a city we love.

I have known Steve for almost as long as I have had Canvas Creek Team Building. He was an early adopter, allowing me to take his team through the process when they needed to bond and change. Over the years, he and I developed agendas for several team events, and he hired me to work with his board of directors, again collaborating on the plans. Steve knows his people, is diligent about giving them what they need to do their work, and likes to control the conversation. Not in a demanding "My way or the highway" sort of style, but with the kind wisdom of "This is where we are going, and this is how we are going to get there" sort of way. As I think of him now, Steve holds many of the characteristics of a Quiet Leader.

Big Sky EDA is one of the most powerful forces for service and growth in our city, and to say I work with them in even the most peripheral way feels like an honor. It is humbling to intimately know the journey they have taken, the personal and professional growth that they have experienced. Especially Steve. He has grown into a confident, respected leader, one who serves before asking and whispers instead of beating a drum, a true Quiet Leader whom I admire and felt I knew after all those events.

Not until we had been standing on that corner for several weeks, in groups both large and small, did I realize that before these gatherings, I didn't know the real Steve.

It is risky for a public official to stand on their faith, to display it to the masses. No one ever doubted that Steve was a man of God (he conducts himself as a man of faith), but he never led a press conference with the fact either. But I watched as week after week, people who respected Steve stood with him and offered their prayers, never judging how someone else believed or what made the person next to us tear up. During these gatherings, I grew from a woman who had never prayed out loud, had shirked the responsibility to lead grace before a meal even, into someone who proudly, publicly offered her words to God and those assembled. And, as I grew, so did Steve. I watched him become more himself, to relax into the fact that his quest to pray for our city with friends, and foes even, allowed him to live both halves of his life as a whole.

Steve seemed to meld the stoic, public Steve with the warm private man of faith and, in the process, help us, the faithful Friday prayer offerers, to do the same ourselves. It wasn't in telling us how to behave or even showing us; it was by quietly turning to his faith when the world had gone mad and asking us to do the same, beside him, on a corner, in downtown Billings.

I am glad he did that, just as I am glad so many others have shown me their hearts, their faith, their leadership, in quiet ways over the years .

As they say, if you pray, pray, and if you sing, sing.

You are a leader, a quiet one, who knows yourself better than anyone else. If, like Steve and me, you sometimes hide your heart, know that it is okay to step into both halves that make you a whole, as long as you do it with grace, and with the purpose of helping your fellow humans. That is what a Quiet Leader named Steve taught me.

And that, Quiet Leader, is what I hope you find yourself doing. Offering whatever you have to give to whoever shows up in front of you needing it. You never know who they might become because you take the time to whisper "You can do it"…

I have been struggling with how to end this book. I keep finding one more example of Quiet Leadership and then another, and I just keep writing and writing, knowing that once you start looking for acts of kind and quiet world-changing leadership, you just keep finding more. Then, while talking to a man who was hiring me to speak at his conference, a man who loved his work raising young leaders, I told him my story and knew at that moment that the end starts with the beginning, which is probably a pretty good leadership lesson on its own. Still, I'll save that for a blog or article; it is time to end this book with my beginning.

When I was a student, no one seemed to have much hope for me. I wasn't the most troublesome student, I was by no means the best student, and I was quiet enough just to overlook. Then Mr. Doubek came into my life. He was the most irreverent, easygoing English teacher I ever had, and he saw something in me, I guess because he teased me in class (lovingly), and he encouraged me to study, to write, and to be funny. By writing a famous quote on the board every day and telling us inappropriate jokes when we were bored, he helped me fall in love with words and the idea of being a bit more me. As I evaluate my style, I realize that I learned it from Mr. Doubek: good content and a joke or two wow most audience members. I couldn't just walk out of his class and into the life I lead now; no, I had to learn one lesson after the next, pursue one course of study and then another, meet individuals and groups, and become me, one Next at a time, which is the story I tell in my book *What's Next.*

Along the way, because I couldn't say no, I was elected PTA president of my daughter's school in Rapid City, South Dakota. She had been at the school for about two months of the second semester, and I had been to two or three PTA meetings. Honestly, I had no idea what I was saying yes to, but I know now that often organizations are so desperate for help that any life raft floating by looks pretty darn appealing, even one with a slow leak. Besides the fact we wanted to move back to Alaska as soon as a promising job opened up for Paul, my slow leak was the fact I didn't want to speak to more than three people at a time, as I'd lock up in fear and stand there crying. PTA presidents get to do a fair amount of public speaking, most of it selling others on the idea of working on a project or donating money. Asking for money was definitely not in my wheelhouse, so if I was going to be a life raft, I wasn't going to save many souls, that was for sure.

My father-in-law, Don Grosz, was a bold man with a gregarious personality. If he walked into a room where he knew no one, he'd walk out with a dozen new friends. I think. I could never test this theory because I never saw him in a room where he didn't know someone. He was that guy. He was also unafraid to tell it like he saw it, or to remind people that chewing gum made them look like idiots, or go to bed when he was ready, leaving guests wondering if it was something they said. With his booming voice, Don told me I'd better grow up and learn to speak in public if I was, in any way, going to have a hope of being a successful PTA president. If I felt a bit honored by the task bestowed on me, he popped the bubble of ego with a withering glance. Don also had a solution in mind, Toastmasters. He also, of course, knew the local club president and got me an invite for the meeting held the next day.

This particular Toastmasters Club met at a local bank, in the boardroom, the type of place I'd never been before. I wore thrift-store clothes and a nervous smile, and tried to hide in a room of extroverted people determined to help others shine, not hide. Because I was Don Grosz's daughter-in-law, I had ready-made fans welcoming me with open arms. There was laughter, extemporaneous one-liners, and a program designed to help me plug a few of the holes in my life raft.

On my third week of attendance, before I knew how to say no, I was slotted to give my first, get-to-know-you speech. It was supposed to be one to two minutes long and share the facts that made me a fascinating human. I didn't feel I had any, at least none I wanted to share. (*Hi, I ran away with Don's son a few years ago, we have a six-year-old daughter, we lived in Alaska till the oil bust ruined that, and I am scared as shit.* That didn't seem quite right.)

When I walked to the podium, everything shut down. I couldn't breathe, I could barely move, and I couldn't see clearly. This was in the days before panic attacks were recognized as part of the norm, but it sure as anything was a panic attack. The last speech I could remember giving was as a junior in high school, and it brought down the house. I didn't intend for it to bring down the house; I intended to tell the story of being a counselor at a camp for special needs kids during the summer. I never felt more needed than at that camp and I felt like my life's work would be to help special needs individuals live their best lives. This was in the days before political correctness, and before the kinder, gentler terms for special needs humans. I hadn't read my speech to anyone before I stepped to the front of the room and opened by saying, "This summer, I went to a camp for retarded kids."

Insert uproarious laughter.

Insert tears.

I didn't even know for sure what they were laughing about; I had, in fact, *gone* to that camp. Then a heckler in the front row said, "We always knew you were retarded, Nelson." I ran out of the room crying, vowing never to give a speech again, and later that year, I ran away with Don Grosz's son. I assume this helps you understand why I started to cry as soon as I got to the Toastmaster podium.

But here is what happened, probably one of the most beautiful acts of kindness that ever happened to me. As I stood there, for an eternity that probably lasted three seconds, two men, who sat on opposite sides of the table, both of whom were wearing three-piece suits and undoubtedly felt at home in the boardroom, stood up, walked behind me at the podium, and put their hands on my back, one on each shoulder blade. One man whispered that I could do it, and crying, I gave the first, and worst, speech of my adult life.

And there was applause.

And they asked me to do it again the following week.

This was unbelievable. These people, skilled orators, brilliant professionals, not only applauded my effort, but they wanted to hear from me again. Can you imagine what that did for me? It was liberating, intoxicating, and the spark I needed to start my career.

I'd like to tell you that I walked to the podium for speech two and stole the show. I did not. I cried, and two men had their hands on my shoulder blades. As customary, there was applause and an invitation to speak again a few weeks later. That time I didn't cry. I didn't need gentlemen propping me up. I got through the entire four-minute speech feeling like I could handle being president of the PTA, which was interesting timing because shortly after that, we moved back to Alaska for the promising job that finally materialized. I assume that as I sat in the principal's office, crying from embarrassment, she was secretly relieved I would not be the PTA president.

When I think of ending with the beginning, it is because of these men—two strangers who supported a young crying mom through her first speech—that every professional success has happened. To this day, when butterflies storm my stomach before a speech, I take a deep breath and can feel the warmth of their hands on my back. When I've helped others give their first speeches, at a Toastmasters meeting, or on a different stage, I have placed my hands on their back and whispered, "You can do it," before applauding like crazy for their effort. And now, when I say something that makes the audience laugh at me, I laugh too, and I move on with what I am trying to say without shedding a tear, happy that my imperfections make me perfectly me.

All of this because two gentlemen, who probably knew Don Grosz but had nothing in common with Karen Grosz, knew that I could be more and supported my most feeble attempt to grow into me with whispered encouragement and warm hands on my back.

If that is not Quiet Leadership, I don't know what is.

I don't know how to say this humbly, but seldom does a day go by that someone, somewhere does not reach out to me to tell me how my words, my work, my silly Monday videos have improved their lives, given them insights, laughs, or more importantly hope for tomorrow. I treasure each of those messages, and I know, as we come to the end of this book, the book I am the most excited to offer to the world, that none of it would have happened if those men, whose names I long ago forgot, had not supported me at that podium. They acted as Quiet Leaders, not looking for glory, not with lectures or an admonishment to do better. They offered the kindest, most humble thing they had to offer, their quiet encouragement, and the warmth of their support, to a woman who needed it so she could live her best life.

Because of their support I have coached, and hopefully inspired, thousands of people both individually and in teams. I have consulted firms as large as Walmart, and been part of decisions to cut, expand and refine millions of dollars worth of community services. I have written letters of recommendation for students who are now doctors, and written these words to help you be a better leader, to impact the world with your gifts, because someone who didn't even know me, offered me support when I needed it most.

And that, Quiet Leader, is what I hope you find yourself doing.

I hope you offer whatever you have to give to whoever shows up in front of you needing it. You never know who they might become because you take the time to whisper, "You can do it" and then applaud for them as a kind and giving Quiet Leader.

Thank you for taking this journey with me, for reading these words, and thinking about your role as a Quiet Leader. I hope you impact the world in meaningful and gigantic ways. K.

Please consider leaving a review on Amazon, or Google, if you enjoyed this book.

Join Karen Grosz's Community to tell your stories of Quiet Leadership and to receive further inspiration.

https://karen-groszs-community.mn.co

Or check in at QuietLeadership.group

UNEXPECTED AND APPRECIATED

I have been blessed beyond belief by people who are kind to me, support me, and do more for me than I could ever thank them for, or do in return. Many are virtual strangers, some dear friends, and some I hug even if I can't recall their name, all of them are Facebook friends. When I asked for 25 people to join my launch group, 94 jumped in within minutes. They read pages of this book that hadn't been edited or proofread, and they gave me a gracious boost of confidence because of their reviews and pre-orders.

I am forever grateful and forever in their debt. It seems like the least I can do to list their names here, in big bold letters, because they are that important, that inspiring to me.

I also want to extend special thanks to Amy Handy for editing, Melaine Fabrizius for the final cover, Matthew Struck for cover inspiration, and Paul Mossberg for valuable insights. Kris Rocky and Sheridan Cotrell stepped in as valued advisors and Bill Schomburg who placed the first bulk order of Quiet Leadership, together, with unexpected and appreciated support you made this project a reality. Without these people and their belief in me, I would have put out a less than satisfactory product. Finally, Andrew Newman reminded me, just when I needed it, that I am a badass and should finish the damn project.

I am honored, humbled and full of tears as I think of what these people did to support Quiet Leadership.

And now, the launch team!

Adelle Coombs
Amanda Stonerock
Amy Handy
Andrea Pluhar
Andrew Newman
Angie Stiller
Annette Welhaven
Ashley Delp
Avery Scully
Barbara Cromwell
Becky Taylor
Beth Montpas
Bill Schomburg
Bridgette Schwebach
Brittany Lane
Brittany Oblander
Candy Carmin
Carla Barker
Cathy Cullen-Kuhr
Cathy Grider
Clementine Lindley
Danny Wyrwas
Debbie Bailey
Debra Ivey
Denise Johnson Smith
Donna Lyn Watson
Donna Smith
Donna Zaharko-
Harrell

Doug Wilson
Dr. Kimberly Meier
Dr. Laura Harbolt
Dr. Victoria Arneson
Elizabeth Terrel
Genia Waller
Heather Ohs
Heidi Davey
Jacqueline Robinson
Jami Clark
Jane Krizek
Jasmine Hansen
Jeanne Goskie
Jeff Rosenberry
Jennifer Fogerty
Jennifer Reiser
Julie Koerber
Justin Sian
Kara Hochhalter
Karin Dawson
Kat Hobza
Kate Knels
Kate ODriscoll
Kathi Lee
Kelly Cresswell
Kelly MacCandless
Kelly Mountain Sheep
Kerry Crowe
Keth Hart

Kim Etzel

Kim Lewis

Kimber Vanatta

Kimberly Hansen

Kitty Aman

Kris Rocky

Kristie Halander

Kristin Peterman

Kristin Smith

Kristin Thomson

Kristy Savaria

Lani Gershmel

Laurie Nelson

Leah Geck

Lesleigh Pagan

Lori Whillock

Lynda Joyce

Makayla Wille

Malia Welhaven

Marcy Lowe

Mary Rutherford

Matt Bartenhagen

Melanie Schwarz

Michaela Morey

Michele Neale

Michelle Luce

Mike Craighill

Nina Shaw

Patty Ceglio

Patty Webster

Paul Mossberg

Paula Poehls

Penny Ronning

Penny Walker

Roseann Santapaola

Sam Whitehead

Sandy Calame

Sara McLean

Sara Romero

Sarah Beth Wald

Sarah Hudson

Sarah Townley

Sarah Vivian

Serena Anderson

Shayla Brown

Sheridan Cotrell

Sherry Moore

Shirley Wicks

Stefanie Hansen

Steven Peterman

Susan Hulsey

Susan Lubke

Tara Balcom

Tegan Schlarman

Tina Roberts

Vayla Thomas

Join us on the Mighty Network,
Karen Grosz's Community!

Now, go lead! Quietly.

Printed in Great Britain
by Amazon

34310417R00138